Polar Animals

ALWIN PEDERSEN

Polar Animals

Translated from the French by
GWYNNE VEVERS

TAPLINGER PUBLISHING CO., INC.
New York

First published in the United States, 1966

TAPLINGER PUBLISHING CO., INC.
29 East Tenth Street
New York, New York 10003

© *Horizons de France* 1958

English translation © *George G. Harrap & Co. Ltd* 1962

Library of Congress Catalogue Card Number: 66-20234

Printed in Great Britain

Author's Preface

T HE TIME has passed when the polar regions were considered to be impenetrable wastes of ice and snow, closed to all but a handful of men. This change is due both to the enterprise of man and to his technical progress. Old prejudices have disappeared in the face of reality. Arctic countries, once visited only by costly expeditions, are now in regular touch with the civilized world, and are arousing growing interest.

North-east Greenland is one of those regions of the Arctic which have in recent years attracted increasing attention, particularly on account of their impressive scenery. It is an area with all the most typical characteristics of the High North, and one which has, in addition, an unequalled Arctic fauna.

My knowledge of North-east Greenland and its fauna is based on a total stay of six years in the area. At first my interest was held by the land mammals—animals which are essentially the most characteristic of the Arctic regions. Among the birds, I have written about only the most typical species. A study of all the birds of North-east Greenland would be beyond the scope of this book, because, with the exception of a single species, none of them are permanent residents. The

commonest species are, however, of great interest, because, in one way
or another, they play an important rôle in the animal life of the Arctic.
I have tried to describe this life as dispassionately as possible in a book
which is at once popular and scientific, and I have added a number of
photographs taken during my time in Greenland.

A.P.

Contents

Illustrations

Map

North-east Greenland

IMAGINE A landscape of dark mountains, rounded and not very high, cut by large valleys and spotted here and there with patches of snow. Such will be your first impression of North-east Greenland when you arrive there on a clear summer day.

The first landing is, however, rather deceptive. When I first stepped ashore, not far from Cape Swainson, on the south coast of Liverpool Land, I found myself literally on a heap of pebbles. The beach was a mass of large white boulders, and there was not the least trace of life. A little farther on some puny lichens and mosses sought a miserable existence among the stones. A bleached reindeer antler bore sole witness that an animal had lived here, although even this was difficult to believe. As far as the eye could see it seemed as though an earthquake had turned the earth upside down, and I must admit to strange feelings at the sight of this godforsaken desert of stone.

This impression must, however, be modified at once. When you get to the other side of the coastal chain the appearance of the country changes. Little by little the desert soil becomes covered with patchy vegetation, though still poor, and thick cushions of green moss edge the streams which the melting snows have formed. The dwarf Arctic

willow, incredibly accommodating, grows wherever a scrap of soil has
collected between the stones or in the rock crevices, and on looking
more closely you can find some thin grass. This miserable vegetation
suffices to nourish a variety of animals.

As you go inland the flora varies according to the region, and depends
on the type of soil, the degree of humidity, and the amount of protection available against the winter storms. Where the original rock comes
to the surface there are growths of crowberry and dwarf willow, and
at a distance of some twelve to eighteen miles from the coast the crowberry completely covers the earth. In the outer part of Scoresby Sound
the large stretches of crowberry recall the heathlands of Jutland. The
willow, the dwarf birch, and the Greenland bilberry, while not forming the thick carpets of the crowberry, become taller and more abundant as you go towards the interior. True willow scrub is rare, and I
myself have seen it only in the inner part of Scoresby Sound, near the
great central glacier which is known as the 'Inland Ice.' This scrub,
some four inches high, forms a belt 20 yards wide half-way up a hillock
about 320 feet high. The trunks of the willows were as thick as a
broom-handle, and careful examination showed them to be more than
a hundred years old. This was the most luxuriant type of vegetation I
saw in North-east Greenland, and is probably restricted to the southern-
most part of that region.

Grass is dominant in places with a substratum of sandstone—as in
Jameson Land and Hochstetter Foreland, where there are grassy areas
quite near the coast. The largest grassy area I have seen is in Jameson
Land, close to Point Constable, which is near Hurry Inlet. The grass
there was so high that it completely hid the head of a musk-ox. Crowberry may also grow quite commonly on the sandstone.

In general the most flourishing vegetation is round the complex of the
three fjords—Scoresby Sound, King Oscar Fjord, and Emperor Franz
Josef Fjord. From there it diminishes gradually towards the north,
at the same time becoming poorer from the edge of the Inland Ice

Page 17. *Ice off the coast of North-east Greenland.*

towards the coast. But far from being homogeneous near the Inland Ice, the vegetation gives way in places to rocks or soil recently freed from the ice, on which vegetation will only very slowly take hold, or which may remain completely bare owing to exposure to the winter gales.

It would be wrong to think that only the most developed plants are attractive to the herbivores. They are eaters, not of willows or high grasses, but of the sparse vegetation, and for this reason the lands bordering the Inland Ice are poor in animals. In the regions where the Inland Ice is so far from the sea that the maximum difference in vegetation is found, it is roughly in the centre of the zone that the herbivores are most numerous. From there they become rarer towards the glacier on the one hand, and towards the coast on the other, although more numerous in the latter direction.

Cold and darkness claim the first month of the year. The earth is wrapped in its shroud of snow, fjords, bays, and lakes are ice-bound, and storms from north and north-east often prevent even man from remaining in the open. While the marine animals can live hidden and well protected under the ice of the fjords, the land mammals have to exist as they may. The lemming and the ermine in their shelters under the snow have much the best lot. The fox and the wolf, on the other hand, wander without rest, searching for food on land, along the coast, and on the ice, and lying up in some sheltered spot when snowstorms threaten. In times of need the fox eats from the stores it has accumulated during the summer as an insurance against winter shortage, but the wolf has to make do with carrion or with anything it is lucky enough to catch. There is no doubt that it must often suffer cruel privation.

Arctic hares gather together in groups high up in the mountains where there are areas free from snow. There they seem to find food quite easily, and can shelter from the storms in the cracks of rocks and

Page 18. *The Devil's Fort in Franz Josef Fjord, one of the typical mountain formations of North-east Greenland.*

under large boulders. The only animals which allow the terrible Arctic weather to rage around them are the musk-ox, which gather in herds in exposed places where the violence of the storms prevents the snow from remaining. In really bad weather they mass together into tight groups with the young animals in the middle. They may browse a little, but mainly they exist on the reserves of fat accumulated during the summer.

The polar bear spends the first month of the year in a hole which it has dug in the snow, or it may go to the open water off the coast and hunt seals. The birds are represented only by ptarmigan, which are, however, quite scarce, as most of them have moved a little southward at the start of the polar night. It is only in the region of Scoresby Sound that they occur in largish numbers, forming flocks which live in the same places as the Arctic hares. Farther to the south there are also ravens, whose conditions of existence are comparable with those of the wolves.

February is marked by the return of the sun, which, in the south, appears over the horizon from January 22, and, in the extreme north, at latitude 81° N., from February 24. This is usually the coldest month of the year, with a mean temperature of $-13°$ F. ($-25°$ C.). There is no marked change in the animal life apart from the return, in the first days of the month, of large flocks of ptarmigan to their former feeding-places. And in her lair beneath the snow the polar bear suckles her cubs.

In March the temperature rises and the snowstorms are less frequent. The early days see the arrival of two other birds, the raven and the snowy owl, and at the end of the month the seals give birth to their young in snow-shelters on the ice. The female polar bears leave their holes of snow, and the males come in from the ice-floes towards the coast and into the fjords to feed on the newborn seals.

Until the second fortnight of April, when the sun rises higher in the sky, it has no apparent effect on the snow. In the warmer hours the snow in exposed places softens and melts. Nevertheless the temperature still remains below 32° F. (0° C.). Snowstorms are few and short in duration, and big changes take place in animal life. Those animals which have passed the winter in large groups now disperse in pairs or in families. In the second half of the month the polar bears mate, and so also do the hares, foxes, ermines, and lemmings. The latter two species leave their burrows under the snow and move about freely. The musk-ox start their wanderings again at the beginning of April, and at the end of the month and in the first days of May the cows have their young. The seals emerge from their holes and lie out on the ice to moult. Early in April comes the first migratory bird, the snow-bunting, which is regarded in Greenland as the harbinger of spring. From then until the end of the month there are arrivals of sea birds, which for a time remain on the edge of the ice off the coast.

The thaw begins in the middle of May, when the maximum temperature rises above 32° F. Places which were thinly covered with snow now have snow-free patches. In the inner parts of the fjords and in the country near the Inland Ice the rivers start to flow once more. Tides break up the floes near the coast, and pools form on the ice. The carnivores start to reproduce, and the female polar bear plays with her cubs and trains them to hunt seals.

In June the thaw reaches its peak. Waters rush down the mountain slopes, bringing with them masses of soil and stone, and much of the low-lying ground is flooded. Night frosts hold back the thaw a little, but only to allow it to start with even greater force the following day. Large gaps appear in the fjord ice off the river-mouths, and the melting snow forms a morass on the floes.

The birds hasten to make the best possible use of the short summer. Those that have mated before arrival in Greenland start to lay their eggs, and by the end of the month all are incubating. The hare, the fox, the lemming, and the ermine now have their young to tend.

At the beginning of July the country is largely free of snow. A belt of open water extends right along the coast, and the ice-floes, eroded by melt-water, start to drift out to sea. At the end of the month most of the fjords and bays are free. Vegetation attains its full growth. From the middle of July onward the young birds begin to appear, while leverets and the young lemmings and ermines start to go about alone.

The musk-ox mate in the second half of the month. Polar cod arrive in shoals from the Arctic Ocean and enter the fjords, where they are hunted by seals and narwhals, and the polar bears begin to move out again on to the ice-floes.

Although the summer reaches its peak in the first fortnight of July, the climate is not really summery until August, when the sky is clear and the temperature agreeable. The winter ice has now disappeared completely, although occasional icebergs from the polar current may enter a fjord and block the mouth. Most of the plants have ceased flowering and wither in the second half of the month. The rich bird life of the summer ebbs; many species moult in privacy, while others leave the country quietly and unnoticed. The musk-ox renews the layer of fat on which it will live during the winter, and the walrus comes ashore to moult, or may even do so out on the floating ice.

Night frosts increase, and the summer ends suddenly at the beginning of September—a month in which the mean temperature falls to below 32° F. In the first days the weather may still be fine, but towards the middle of the month the squalls of autumn are suddenly let loose. The last migratory birds depart, and once more one is left alone in the desolation of winter.

The first big fall of snow does not occur generally before the middle of October, and by this time there is scarcely any open water to be seen. The musk-ox gather together in their winter quarters, the foxes come down to the coast, and the lemmings and ermines prepare their burrows under the snow. At the same time the seals form air-holes in the still-thin ice, which they will enlarge in the course of the winter.

In latitude 81° N. the sun disappears on October 19, and in Scoresby Sound on November 21. The months of November and December scarcely differ from the first month of the year. From now on the polar night reigns over Greenland.

The Musk-ox

MUSK-OX were first recorded in a book entitled *Relation du détroit et de la baie d'Hudson*, by the French trapper Jérémie, which was published in 1720. He described an animal resembling a bison: "There is a kind of ox which we named musk-ox on account of its strong smell of musk, which makes it quite inedible at certain times of the year."

Such was the first occurrence of the musk-ox in the literature. It was first reported for North-east Greenland in *The Second German North Polar Expedition*, a book written by one of the members of the German expedition which spent the winter of 1869–70 on Sabine Island. This author writes:

> On Shannon Island we had climbed a peak about 250 feet high and were making a beacon there, when in the distance we saw a large and peculiar animal which resembled neither a bear nor a reindeer. At the time we did not think of the musk-ox, which had never been observed in North-east Greenland, and so were quite astounded when we saw this creature in front of us. We immediately started off in pursuit of it, and Peter Iversen succeeded in killing it. Later on we found that musk-ox lived along the whole coast up to latitude 77° N. (the most northerly point reached by the

expedition during a sledge journey in 1870). We often saw herds with up
to sixteen animals in the valleys and on the slopes of the mountains. It was
remarkable that their numbers seemed to increase up to 77° N., but
diminished as we went south. The reindeer,[1] on the other hand, showed
exactly the opposite distribution, for we never found a single one north
of 75° N.

About fifty years before the Germans made this observation the
same territory was first explored by two Englishmen, Clavering and
Sabine. It is curious that neither of them saw any trace of musk-ox.
In the course of a reconnaissance of an island at the entrance of Loch
Fyne which now bears his name Sabine touched land at several places,
notably the island which he named after Clavering and the head of the
fjord, which are now among the best musk-ox localities. In view of the
fact that musk-ox leave very obvious tracks, it is quite possible that
at this period they did not live at all in North-east Greenland, or else
that they were very rare there. The remains of Eskimo settlements in
the area also support this conclusion, for they contain no bones of the
musk-ox. As these Eskimos lived entirely by hunting they would
certainly have killed them if they had been there.

We do not know exactly when the Eskimos lived in the area. The
last—indeed, the only ones—were seen by Clavering on the south
coast of Clavering Island in the summer of 1823. But the ruins are
previous to this time. Judging from the overgrown state of the houses,
they must be about two hundred years old.

It is only the Eskimos who lived in Germania Land who hunted the
musk-ox in large numbers. Like the Eskimo, this animal originally
came to North Greenland from the north of Canada, travelling over
the frozen ice in winter, and from there it moved on to the east coast.

[1] Up to 1900 reindeer were abundant in the whole of North-east Greenland, except
perhaps in the extreme north. Since then they have disappeared, leaving no trace except
for a few antlers and occasional skeletons of animals which had probably died a natural
death. There is no doubt that they must have migrated elsewhere, probably to West
Greenland. The route they must have taken is not known, but it is quite possible that
they may have crossed part of the Inland Ice. Perhaps we shall never know whether they
reached their destination or perished on the way.

I will discuss later why it should have chosen this difficult route along a coastline reaching almost to the Pole, instead of moving down the west coast, where there are many much more fertile areas.

At first the musk-ox seem to have been restricted to the north-western part of the country, at the northern end of Melville Bay, for it is there that they were found by the first Eskimos who came to Greenland. The ice-free area there is very restricted and scarcely suitable for feeding large herbivores. Quite soon the musk-ox became too numerous for these sparse pastures, and they crossed Peary Land and reached the good grazing of the north-east coast. In this journey they probably passed to the south of Peary Land—that is, at the bottom of Independence Fjord.

The subsequent dispersal of musk-ox on the east coast may be followed in greater detail. At the time when the Eskimos lived along the northern half of this coastline musk-ox extended south to latitude 77° N. At the beginning of the nineteenth century they moved south to 75° N., and beyond that in about 1870. By the end of the century they had invaded Franz Josef Fjord and had reached the north side of Scoresby Sound. Since then the distribution of musk-ox in North-east Greenland has not changed, except in so far as their numbers are concerned. The climatic conditions of the area seem to satisfy their requirements perfectly, and although they have been much hunted, this is the only part of the world where they are still abundant. In Canada, where they originally lived in the Barren Grounds and part of Parry Island, they have almost disappeared, and now live only in the extreme north. They have disappeared from North-west Greenland, where they are thought to have been exterminated by the Eskimos—unless they left as the result of a change in the climate. This point ought to be clarified, for if the Eskimos were responsible, then we ought not to hesitate in reintroducing the musk-ox into a region which is so poor in animal life.

If musk-ox are to prosper they must have a dry, continental-type climate, like that of the northern parts of our hemisphere. In North-east Greenland the southern limit of their range is Scoresby Sound. The present amelioration of the climate is very unfavourable to them, and many have been found dead during recent years. Before this climate change it was estimated that there were about 10,000 head of musk-ox in Greenland and North America.

During winter musk-ox need stretches of grass as far as possible free of snow. They gather together in such places at the beginning of the bad season and remain there until the spring. When these snow-free areas are large the musk-ox will remain on them throughout the year. Most of the snow-free areas are, however, quite small—the sides of a mountain, a high plateau, or a stretch of beach, for instance. Other areas may cover a whole district, and among them are Hochstetter Foreland, Shannon Island, Hudson Land, a great part of Jameson Land, and Germania Land. The latter is the most northern locality with large herds of musk-ox. They live permanently in the grassy area between Saelsö and Mörkefjord. Many of the herds wander to the neighbourhood of the Inland Ice, and sometimes they descend almost as far down as the islands. At intervals they also visit Great Koldewey, but do not remain there. The population of musk-ox in this district is very much dispersed, and most of the animals spend the winter on the higher ground.

The vast complex of Scoresby Sound marks the southern limit of the musk-ox's range. It has been thought that the large snowfields and the Inland Ice in this area have prevented them from spreading farther south—as is supposed to have happened at Melville Bay, on the northwest coast—but I do not now consider that this is the true explanation. Whole herds of musk-ox travel over the Inland Ice when they are searching for new pastures. Besides, to have reached Scoresby Sound at all they must have crossed many snowfields and large, frozen inlets of the sea. To me it seems that one must look for the explanation in the differences of climate north and south of Scoresby Sound. To the south there are often periods in the first half of winter when there is a thaw with rain and high humidity. Thick fogs from the neighbouring

Page 27. *Wordie Glacier.*
Page 28. *Part of the mouth of the magnificent Franz Josef Fjord.*

open water spread over the whole district. Now, the thick, woolly pelt of the musk-ox is a perfect protection against extreme cold, but not against damp. One day of rain or melting snow is enough to soak their fur, and when it freezes again ice forms among the hairs. Other fur animals, such as the wolf, fox, and dog, are exposed to the same hazard, but they can guard against it by licking the fur dry, and even if icicles do form they can break them up with their teeth, but this the musk-ox cannot do. They often shake their fur, but without being able to get rid of the ice. In a humid climate the icicles increase in number and in volume until the animal is no longer able to move properly and becomes an easy prey for its enemies; this does not happen to musk-ox living in a permanently dry and cold climate. In my opinion these are the conditions which limit the spread of musk-ox in Greenland, and which originally caused it to move to the north-east of the country, instead of descending along the west coast, where the winter is as un-stable as in the south-east.

The musk-ox is certainly one of the most peculiar mammals living to-day, and in zoological classification it holds a place apart. At first sight it resembles a bison on account of the powerful shoulders, which form a kind of hump in the adult. At close quarters the thick-set body, the short neck, the horns bent down towards the ground, and especially its way of walking remind one of a sheep, with which it has other characteristics in common, such as the hairy muzzle, the short tail hidden in the fur, the asymmetrical hooves—the outer one rounded, the inner pointed—and the general shape and construction of the skull. On the other hand, the period of gestation, the number of nipples— four and not two, as thought until recently—and certain other ana-tomical characteristics suggest that the musk-ox is not far away from our domestic cattle. This is why zoologists have classified it between sheep and cattle and have given it the Latin name *Ovibos*.

Page 29. *The heavy woolly fleece of the musk-ox is so long that only the white feet appear beneath it.*
Page 30. *An adult male musk-ox.*

Nowadays we recognize three races of musk-ox, of which two, *Ovibos moschatus moschatus* and *Ovibos moschatus niphoecus*, live in North America. Only about 800 animals of these two races still survive. All the other musk-ox belong to the third race, *Ovibos moschatus wardi*, and live in the polar islands north of Canada and in Greenland. This race is distinguished from the others by its smaller size and by the white forehead of the cows and calves.

On average the adult bulls measure four feet two inches to the hump; the cows are a little smaller and less massive. The thick mane which grows along the back makes them look taller than they are. The skin is covered with a soft wool and, outside it, by the fleece, which falls from the back to a few inches above the hooves, and completely envelops the animal like a fringed rug. The colour is brown, but from a distance and especially against snow it appears almost black. The frizzled mane on the nape of the neck and on the shoulders is a little paler in colour; in very old males it may be completely brown. In the middle of the back there is a light, saddle-shaped patch, which is yellowish or almost white in old males. In the cows and calves there is a white area between the horns, which disappears in the adult males because their horns grow together at the bases to cover the forehead completely. The parts of the legs which are visible beneath the fleece are white.

In their first year the calves carry a short woolly coat. It is only at the beginning of the second winter that they grow the mantle of true hairs, which is never moulted and remains the same in summer and in winter. It is only the underlayer of wool which is renewed. At the beginning of winter this wool thickens and elongates, and lifts the outer fleece, which thus has the appearance of greater thickness. In spring, at the end of April or the beginning of May, the wool becomes detached and works its way up gradually to the surface, where its grey, mossy colour shines in the sunlight. In order to rid themselves of this wool the animals rub against rocks and blocks of ice. In the heart of the summer and even in autumn old males are often still covered with this discoloured wool, which hangs in long tassels from their sides, giving them an appearance of great age. This condition of the fleece has often been erroneously described as a winter coat.

The most striking features of the musk-ox are the horns. They cover the forehead with a thick shield, with a groove in the middle, bend downward on each side of the head, and then curve up again with the point facing downward. They are dangerous weapons. The horns of the cows are less powerful at the base and smaller, and they do not cover so much of the forehead. A male is adult in his fifth year; before this his horns are not sufficiently developed for him to fight other males. The cows are capable of reproduction in their third year.

Musk-ox live in herds, and solitary animals are usually old males which have mostly been herd-leaders until they were dispossessed by a stronger rival. Certain of these old bulls may sometimes succeed in regaining the leadership of a herd, but the majority of them are fated to wander, solitary, for the rest of their days. They may take refuge on the islands in the fjords, but they are usually on the move. One meets them even on the nunataks[1] in the Inland Ice. Sometimes two or three of these unfortunates unite to afford mutual protection against danger, with one of them playing the rôle of leader. But this apparent solidarity disappears in the mating season, when they fight one another as though they were still trying to gain possession of a herd.

A herd usually consists of an adult bull, with two or three cows and their calves, but it may be larger. The biggest herd I have ever seen had twenty-two animals. The herd rarely contains more than four cows, the remainder being young animals and calves, with an adult male as leader. He is responsible for the security of his family, gathers them together on the approach of danger, and is the first to attack and the last to flee. On the pastures and during their migrations the cows and calves move first, then the other young animals which may wander out on each side, and finally the bull, fifty to a hundred yards to the rear. In this way he can keep them all in view and watch if any of the youngsters move too far away. When the herd is resting and chewing the cud he still keeps sufficiently far away to be able to watch for

[1] Mountain summits emerging from the Inland Ice not far from its edge.

danger, or, in the mating season, to see whether any rival approaches to challenge him.

It is usually the cows which choose the migration routes. If they come to an obstacle, such as a deep river-bed, a crevasse, or a steep cliff, which they cannot pass they wait for the leader. He examines the position, and then, quietly and deliberately, descends the ravine or wades through the torrent. Once he has crossed the worst part the cows follow, but when they have very young calves they search for an easy route, and if the bull tries to lead them along a route that is dangerous they will refuse to follow, and he has to retrace his steps. The cows always avoid large rivers.

In rough country the herds always follow the same routes, moving along paths which climb towards the plateau and along the snowfields, crossing the valleys and descending to the coasts. In following these routes they sometimes reach high up towards the steep summits.

One could scarcely say that the musk-ox has a lively temperament. A travelling herd gives an impression of a group of astonishingly phlegmatic creatures. The adults march as though in deep meditation, and it seems as though nothing could upset their composure. If anything catches their attention they will stop and slowly lift their heads. Their bearing gives one the impression of quiet superiority. They show no sign of disturbance even when they meet an enemy face to face. In situations where any other wild animal would immediately tense its muscles, ready to spring, a musk-ox makes only a slow, dignified movement. One never sees them rush at an obstacle. When they have to cross a torrent they will submerge up to the chest rather than look for a narrow place to clear by leaping. Nevertheless, they can move fast—faster, in fact, than would be expected of an animal so burdened with heavy fur—but they do so only when pressed. They never trot, but when, exceptionally, they find it necessary to take flight they put in a short gallop which gives them a remarkable turn of speed.

I can say little of their sense of smell, which certain explorers have regarded as acute. Because of their normal phlegmatic temperament it is difficult to say whether they first become aware of danger at the

moment they raise their heads or whether they have already scented it
long before. From my own experience, based on innumerable en-
counters in the most diverse circumstances, I have the impression that
they rely more on sight than on smell.

Further evidence of their reserved behaviour is the fact that one
rarely hears the voice of the adult, which resembles the bellowing of a
bull. The calves, on the other hand, often bleat just like sheep, especially
when they are being hunted and the cows are no longer able to defend
them.

Except in the great musk-ox areas such as Hochstetter Foreland,
Shannon Island, Hudson Land, and Jameson Land, where the good
living conditions allow them to be more sedentary, the herds usually
move in summer to areas which were thickly covered in snow during
the winter. These are regular migrations, with the herds coming in
from the surrounding areas during the spring and disappearing in the
course of the autumn.

By the beginning of the Arctic night the herds are back in their
winter quarters, and where space is short they combine into larger
units. In places where a sedentary population is augmented by animals
from elsewhere the bulls form groups on their own of twenty to fifty
head. During the whole of the dark period they remain in a restricted
area. They move about so little that one can easily find them again at
the end of the winter night. They start to wander again only about
two weeks after the return of the sun, but yet another month passes
before they form up again into individual herds and start to move off.

The musk-ox is the only land mammal of the High North which can
endure the full severity of the Arctic winter. When the country is swept
by bitter snowstorms for days at a time the musk-ox tolerates the full
blast, while all other living things, including the polar bear, have disappeared into shelter. Even the worst tempests do not seem to worry
them, and I believe that, in general, they do not suffer so much from
the cold as they do from the heat in summer. The first-year calves are,
however, insufficiently protected by their short woolly coats, and they
do need the protection of their elders. This is probably one of the

reasons why musk-ox assemble in large groups in winter. They choose
a spot where the snowstorms blow in a constant direction, and form a
circle with their heads facing the wind. The old males are always at the
most exposed place, where their tall humps help to protect the others.
The youngsters stand in the centre; they could scarcely be better protected than behind this wall of fur. These groups remain standing in
this way for days on end without lying down. When the storm is at
its worst the musk-ox close up into a compact, wedge-shaped mass, of
which the point is formed by two bulls which face head into wind.

Musk-ox feed principally on Arctic willow and grass, but when
necessary they will eat almost any other plant. During the summer
when there is plenty of food they graze continuously night and day
without stopping. They pause to chew the cud only when their stomachs are full, or, in the heat of midday, to seek the freshness of a
patch of snow. In this way they build up the layer of fat which, in
autumn, gives them a portly appearance, and which is so necessary if
they are to get through the winter without becoming too weak. At the
end of the polar night they are still in quite good shape—a condition
which is also the result of their sedentary life during this period. It is
after this that they quickly become very thin. In the second half of
May—that is, just before the new crop of plants appears—the cows
look as though they have shrunk to half-size.

In the extreme north of Greenland the sudden onset of frost at the
beginning of winter freezes the still-living vegetation and preserves a
major part of its nutritive value during the whole of the bad season.
To the south of Germania Land I have seen this phenomenon high up
in the mountains, but never on low-lying ground—in particular never
in the musk-ox areas, where the vegetation has time to wither before it
is frozen. The musk-ox which live there must therefore put up with
very poor food during the whole of the winter, and they would be
quite unable to survive without the fat reserve accumulated during
the summer. In spring the musk-ox come down again, still in large
groups, towards the lower regions, which have been covered in snow
during the winter, and five or six weeks after the return of the sun they

break up again into individual herds. Even though mating does not occur until two months later (July and August), the bulls are already becoming bellicose. Now is the time when the young males and the solitary bulls have a chance to dispute the right of the herd-leaders to retain their property. When there are several young adult males in the same herd they often leave it, followed by one or more heifers, and form new families.

The fighting looks as though it starts as a game. The rival animals come face to face, and then quite suddenly move past each other peacefully. A little later they may become irritated again, and this time more seriously. The struggle is extremely primitive in character. It is just a trial of force, devoid of all cunning and ingenuity, but it serves to show the enormous strength possessed by these animals. In areas with large populations of musk-ox one can see many skirmishes in the spring, but rarely decisive fights. Often the solitary bulls will try their luck against the superior herd-leaders, and generally they are chased off after the first encounter, happy to be able to withdraw until they meet the next herd. Condemned from their youth to wander solitarily, they tramp around hoping to find a herd without a leader, or to be able to drive off an old leader which has become weakened by age. When a large bull goes solitary it is usually at an age when he has finally given up trying to be the leader of a herd. He may still, however, like to be followed by one or more smaller bulls for whom he plays the rôle of protector.

A bull still in full vigour may also lose his position as leader, either by being dispossessed by a more powerful rival, or by being separated from his cows by hunters, or through some other accident. If this happens in winter or in early spring he may move off on his own, but as the rutting season approaches he becomes restless, is ceaselessly on the move, trying to satisfy his desire to fight by scraping the earth with his horns and feet and attacking anything he meets. A bull in this state is as dangerous as a walrus at sea. As soon as he has scented a herd he will not rest until he has provoked the owner. It is a hard combat, for the latter has to face an adversary of the same size as himself, who refuses to be chased away at the first encounter, and who may even become the victor.

I was once a witness of this in Liverpool Land. Both bulls were astonishingly tenacious, and they seemed to be of the same strength. Their dark manes and the good state of their horns suggested that they were both relatively young. One had a herd of eight beasts; the other was alone. When I first saw them the solitary bull was lying behind a small hill about fifty paces from the herd. The leader was standing up, doubtless keeping an eye on the intruder, but both gave an impression of complete indifference. They looked at each other for a moment, and then went on grazing. One of the cows got up, and the leader tried to cover her, but gave up when he saw the other bull approaching. Slowly and with measured step the leader walked down the slope and stopped twenty paces from his adversary. For a moment both stood motionless examining each other, and then it seemed as though they exerted a mutual attraction. Each lifted its head to shoulder height, with the muzzle resting on the chest, and with the neck and shoulders arched like those of a circus horse, in such a way that the heavy frontal shield of horn was fully presented.

In this symmetrical and decorative stance they looked like two enormous rams. Suddenly, as though at a given signal, they both took the weight on to their hindquarters and rushed at each other. The shock was so violent that I could hear it as a dull thud from where I was watching a hundred yards away. They rested for a moment face to face, then retreated to their original positions and again threw themselves at each other. They repeated these assaults for half an hour, stopping only once to rub their horns against some boulders. Then they had a little pause for grazing, but still remained facing each other. In less than five minutes they started again as suddenly as they had stopped. Little

Page 39. *A young musk-ox calf.*
   A typical musk-ox family. It consists of the leader (to the left), two cows, each with a one-year-old calf, and a heifer.
Page 40. *In summer the musk-ox seek the freshness of a patch of snow.*

by little the solitary bull seemed to be finding difficulty in standing up against its opponent. At each attack its limbs bent, imperceptibly at first, and then so obviously that defeat seemed inevitable. The last shock pushed it over on to its hindquarters, and while its adversary prepared for a new assault it got up, turned round, and fled. The other bull made a show of pursuing it, and then returned to the herd. The whole fight had lasted for a good hour.

These duels may become bloody. Sometimes one finds skeletons of musk-ox which have died from a fracture of the frontal part of the skull. I have seen one myself, and fur-trappers have told me of two similar cases. The explorer Knud Rasmussen also speaks of a broken skull, which he found at the foot of Independence Fjord. It is, however, only rarely that fights finish in this way.

Rutting starts in the first half of July and goes on into September. The first to come on heat are the heifers and those cows which have not calved during the year; the last are those which are suckling, particularly those which have had two calves in one year. There is no fixed rule about this, however. Most of the matings take place in the first half of August.

A little before the start of the rutting, and for a short period afterwards, the males give off a strong, sweetish smell, which has been compared with that of musk. I do not know how far this comparison is justified, but it is from it that *Ovibos* got the popular name of musk-ox; the young animals also have this smell, but it is less pronounced. In adults the smell is so strong that their flesh is quite inedible at this time of year.

There may be considerable variation in the reproduction of the musk-ox. Up to now it has been thought that the cows had a calf at the most

Page 41. *A herd of musk-ox.*
     Two cows and a male calf preparing to receive an attack.
Page 42. *The pelt of a pure-white Arctic wolf.*
     An Arctic wolf killed in Liverpool Land.

C

in every second year. In actual fact it is not unusual for them to calve every year, and they may even have two calves at a time. On the other hand, two or three years may go by before a cow calves again. It depends on the condition of the mother at the time of mating, and especially on the extent to which she has been able to feed herself during the preceding winter. Conditions in North-east Greenland may vary considerably from year to year. In certain years when the whole country is covered with thick snow, including those areas where it is usually blown away by the storms, the musk-ox have to live right from the beginning of winter on the fat accumulated during the summer. As spring approaches they will have become very thin. The bulls and the young animals can stand this period of famine quite well, but the cows in calf may have suffered so long that they will not have regained their normal strength by the time the following breeding season starts. In such years the number of births is very low.

The period of gestation is about eight and a half months, and the calves are born at the end of April and the beginning of May, although only a few in the latter month, and never later. The calves are able to follow the herd from the second or third day. Cows which still have a calf from the previous year will go on feeding it until some weeks after giving birth to the new calf, and where two years elapse between births the calves are fed for eighteen months.

Musk-ox are well known for their peculiar behaviour in the presence of man. They pay no attention when they see him with a gun. When one approaches them they stop grazing, lift their heads, and at a distance of about twenty paces they will either turn and run away, or they will charge with heads lowered. There is, therefore, a difference between their method of attacking a rival and an enemy of another species. In the latter case they hold the head down between the frontlegs, and then try to impale their victim with the horns. In fact, they will attack man in exactly the same way as they do the wolf—their only enemy among the animals. One can see this when a dog attacks a herd. The adults form a circle round the young animals and then wait. As soon as the dog approaches one of them, usually the leader, makes a sudden sortie. If the dog does not manage to evade the blow it will be thrown into the air and finish up under the sharp hooves of the bull.

I have seen several dogs killed in this way in the Scoresby Sound area. When a herd comes near a Greenlandic settlement all the dogs in the neighbourhood will attack. It is not unusual for several of them to be killed before the Greenlanders have time to intervene. One day there was a herd on a small hill. A Greenlander who was travelling by sledge did not see them until he arrived at the top, and then it was too late to avoid them. The musk-ox rushed forward, and the dogs refused to retreat. The Greenlander only just had time to cut the traces before they met. Three dogs were thrown into the air, but before they had landed the man had killed the leading bull. One of the dogs was killed on the spot, and two others, mortally wounded, crawled towards the sledge, followed by their entrails. A fourth dog died shortly afterwards.

Although the musk-ox can defend itself well against the dog and the wolf, it is really no match for man. Although hunted continually, it is surprising that it has not yet learned that flight is its only safeguard. Doubtless this lack of comprehension indicates a low degree of intelligence. Its principal adaptation is its power to survive in the Arctic climate, and this has had considerable effect on the behaviour of the species. Such extreme specialization almost always involves a loss of other faculties, and may go so far as to prevent a species from adapting itself to some new change in its environment. The musk-ox seems to me to be in this phase of evolution. As far as is possible for a ruminant it has become adapted to the natural conditions of its polar home, but, having done this, it has lost the faculty of dealing with changes in its living conditions. It knows no other natural enemy except the wolf, and this it can deal with perfectly well. On the other hand, it has not become adapted to dealing with man, and when it meets one it can only behave as it would towards a wolf.

Each time I have come across a herd of musk-ox they have shown themselves unable to make a decision; they have not known whether to remain where they were or to flee, and if they have decided to flee it is at a time when they could all have been shot.

When a musk-ox is killed the others are visibly disturbed, especially if it has been the leader. It is quite distressing to see these fine animals standing around the victim as though paralysed, and letting themselves be killed one by one. One cannot really talk of hunting the musk-ox, for it is a slaughter, or what the Norwegian hunters call a butchering. The following two stories show how defenceless these animals are.

Towards the middle of April I had gone with the Danish hunter Ewald Rasmussen to Knudshoved, on the east coast of Hudson Land. We were living in a small hut, and while Rasmussen was hunting foxes in the neighbourhood I made several trips to find out whether there were any musk-ox around.

One day, about ten miles from the hut, I came across a large herd grazing on a hill in a wide valley. Our dogs were short of food, and we had agreed to kill a musk-ox as soon as we could. If we could kill one we could easily transport it by sledge to the coast, and also this seemed a good opportunity to complete my collection of photographs with some close-ups. On account of the weather we could not hunt them until the following day, and we were afraid that they would climb higher during the night, but fortunately we found them again in the same spot.

I had to approach them quite closely, and, as the risk of being attacked thus became greater, we brought along two dogs which had already shown their skill in hunting musk-ox. The dogs would also help to contain the herd if it showed any sign of moving off.

After an hour's walking we were close enough to the animals to see them with the naked eye. There were twenty-one in all, of which three were adult bulls; this confirmed that we were dealing not with a herd, but with a group which had not yet divided up into herds. They were on a slope which was free of snow. Farther up the hill we saw a small herd of five beasts, and at the bottom of the valley two solitary bulls.

It was no longer any use for us to try to hide. The musk-ox scarcely deigned to notice us, even if they had scented us long before. When we were about three hundred yards from them the adults, who had

been lying down, got up and slowly moved down the hill. We were
not more than two hundred yards away when they all stopped grazing
and turned in our direction. By this time we had reached the snow-
free ground, and while we rested to allow them to calm down I
took the opportunity to watch them more closely through my field-
glasses.

The group consisted of three bulls, seven cows, and eleven young
animals. Among the youngsters there was a particularly fine male,
perhaps about five years old, with white horns and a fleece which was
almost black. Most of the other young ones were about two years old,
but there were four calves of the preceding year.

They started to graze again, but they had now moved closer together. We got up, and again they stood motionless and watched us.
When we approached they all retreated in a group, and as they
became restless the bulls assembled the others into a defensive position by nudging them in the hindquarters. Although they seemed to
move slowly, it was surprising how quickly they formed a line with
an old bull at each end. The calves had disappeared in among the
adults.

I asked Rasmussen to stay behind with the dogs while I advanced
to take some photographs. If the beasts either fled or attacked he was
to release the dogs, but, to avoid provoking either of these reactions
before I had taken the photographs, I went forward slowly, stopping
after each step. The musk-ox formed a circle with the young behind
the adults. I approached to a distance of thirty yards. The adult bulls
were now disturbed; they snorted and rubbed their horns with the
inner side of the front legs—a sure sign that they were not going to
turn and run. The bulls always do this before charging. By this means
the long hairs, which cover most of the muzzle from the base of the
horns to the nose, become impregnated with secretion, so that they do
not blow around and cover the eyes during the fight. The secretion
comes from a small gland just below the eyes which produces a fatty
liquid. Sometimes they will also rub the horny frontal shield on the
ground to make its surface rough.

As I was unarmed there was no point in moving in closer, and so I gave a signal to Rasmussen to release the dogs. When the bulls saw their sworn enemies they massed themselves even closer and waited with lowered heads. The dogs avoided a frontal attack and ran round in a circle to approach from the rear. The old bulls tried several sorties against them, but our dogs were old hands, and they avoided them each time. Rasmussen had now come up and was ready to shoot if it should be necessary, in view of my proximity to the bulls. As arranged, he intended to shoot one of them, and his chance was to come quite soon.

I advanced again, and the dogs became bolder. Then the young bull with white horns, which I had already noticed, suddenly slipped through the old males who formed the outer defence, dealt a blow to a dog who was passing, and succeeded in ripping its side. The wounded dog turned and ran howling towards me, with the angry bull in full chase. The whole thing was so sudden and at such close range that I had no chance to escape. Just as the dog reached me Rasmussen took aim and fired. The bull fell, then got up on its feet and started back to the herd; then it fell again and was dead.

All this had a considerable effect on the other beasts. They seemed completely at a loss and tried to entrench themselves behind the dead bull; it was a scene of pitiful confusion. Their lack of decision had never struck me so forcibly before. Slowly and painfully two of the bulls moved to the front of the herd to defend it against a further attack. It was quite evident that the longer we remained, the longer they would, and we were anxious to cut up the dead animal. There was, therefore, nothing we could do but leave the frightened animals in peace, to calm down and perhaps to move off. We recalled the dogs and walked away. An hour later, when we were about half a mile from them, the musk-ox had dispersed and were grazing again, and they seemed to be moving slowly up the hill. We thought they would now let us get to the dead animal, but we were quite mistaken, for they moved towards us at the gallop and formed up again close to the carcass. It was getting quite late, and so we returned to the hut.

By the following day the musk-ox had gone. They had separated into three small herds, but were so far away from the dead animal that they were not disturbed by us. The meat from our victim was now only fit for feeding to the dogs, for musk-ox flesh decomposes very rapidly.

The second hunt took place on Shannon Island. I was there with two Danish hunters, Philbert and Christoffersen. I had arrived with Christoffersen a fortnight before from Hochstetter Foreland, and we had met Philbert near David Gray, where he had been living in a hut for a week and hunting foxes. Our plan had been to travel on the open water along the east coast of Shannon Island, but before setting off for Philipp Brocke, the southern point of the island, we had to remain for a couple of days at David Gray in order to get some dog food for the journey.

Philbert had killed a bull which was grazing about two hundred yards from the hut at the time of his arrival. It was a very old solitary animal, and extraordinarily small and ill-nourished. Its left horn had fallen off, and it was altogether too thin for our dogs, so we decided on a hunt for the following day. We had only to climb a hill behind the hut to get a fine view over the low-lying areas of the islands, and about two and a half miles away we saw a large group of nineteen and a family herd of four musk-ox. Once they had scented us they ran about in little groups of three to five individuals, gathering together and then dispersing, as though unable to decide on a defensive position. Finally, as it looked as though they were going to escape, we let loose the dog. I have never seen a group assemble in such an unusual fashion. There were nine bulls, which were almost adult, and three cows, of which one was very old and larger than normal; she was followed by a small calf which, from the time of year, must have been at least six months old, although it was no taller than a four-month-old calf. The second cow, on the other hand, had two well-developed calves. There were also three young of the preceding year, of indeterminate sex. The other herd, which consisted of an adult bull, a cow with her calf, and a heifer, stood apart on the left wing of the main group. There was apparently no leader in this main group; each time two of the young approached they faced each other head on and exchanged blows. The calves remained out in the open, which is unusual in a group which is on the defensive. The cows tried to hide them, but when menaced by the dog they soon retreated to their first position of defence. Taking advantage of this disorder, I approached to within a few yards of the animals without any of them showing any sign of attacking. At this close range I noticed that they all had icicles in their fur. One cow in particular carried a shield of ice on her back; her calf had pieces of ice as large as a fist festooned on its fur, which clinked every time it moved.

I tried to take some photographs, but the shutter had seized up in the frost: the thermometer registered minus 22° F. (− 30° C.). When I accidentally touched the metal of the camera my skin stuck to it. The photographs which I had taken before had probably been over-exposed, and as I did not want to go back empty-handed I put the camera, balanced on its case, on the snow, in the hope that the sun would thaw it out.

During the quarter of an hour that I remained there the animals were much occupied with their mutual squabbles and took no notice of me. Finally I was ready to photograph them. They still showed no sign of charging. Their apathy even tired the dog, which we were continually trying to call off. During one of the dog's attacks the old cow nudged a bull in the hindquarters to get it to respond. The bull turned sharply, but only to use its strength on its neighbour. Finally another bull lost patience and rushed at the dog. Once he was well away from the rest he was hit by a couple of shots. He turned back towards the herd, and was finally killed by a third shot. The behaviour of his companions seemed quite unaffected, and none of them moved, except a cow, which went over and sniffed at the victim. The total absence of any form of cohesion showed clearly that they were merely

Page 51. *Arctic hares in a winter landscape.*
Page 52. *An Arctic hare, in its summer coat, hiding behind a rock.*
     A leveret.

a random collection, and not a true herd. I knew from experience that if one makes a noise a group of musk-ox will sometimes move off, so we recalled the dog and tried this method, shouting as loudly as we could. At first the musk-ox seemed quite paralysed and forgot their mutual differences; then they started to retreat.

At this moment an amazing thing happened. We were trying to get back our breath, before starting to shout again, when I heard a scraping noise coming from the snowfield above us, but not knowing what it was I didn't mention it to my companions. A moment later, just as we were going to start shouting again, a white animal appeared on the snow. I pointed it out and cried, "A wolf!" Almost at the same time it started to move down at a good pace, and then we saw it was a polar bear.

What would the musk-ox do if the bear approached? We stood quite still so as not to distract its attention. At a single bound it reached the bottom of the snowfield and stood up with head erect. It sniffed twice, so loudly that we could hear it quite distinctly, and seemed to be hesitating between us and the musk-ox, which in the meantime had reassembled on a small hillock about fifty yards from the place where we had attacked them. They were all facing towards the bear. The bulls snorted and sniffed, probably in order to scent this new enemy. After two minutes of reflection the bear turned and ran back along its tracks to the spot from which it had come, and suddenly disappeared in the snow. We later learned that it was a female with two cubs in a den in the middle of the snowfield. Our cries had brought her out of hiding to see what was happening, and—curiosity satisfied—she had returned to her cubs.

Page 53. *Even in summer the Arctic hares retain their winter whiteness. Here at an altitude of 3000 ft. the earth appears bare, but among the stones are the small plants and mosses on which the hares feed in winter.*
Typical 'hare country' in North-east Greenland.

Page 54. *Arctic hares manage to find sufficient food even in stony areas. Their protruding teeth allow them to feed on small plants growing between the stones.*

The musk-ox were now lying down and chewing the cud, and they let us approach the dead male. When we returned on the following day to collect the meat it had been moved about three hundred yards away and was not far from the bear's den.

In the course of time thousands of musk-ox have been killed in Greenland and on the polar islands north of Canada. Since 1917 the Canadian Government has protected these animals on the whole of its mainland territory. Some years later it was made illegal to hunt musk-ox on the islands, so that the species is now totally protected in North America. From 1951 onward there has been partial protection in Greenland. Hunters who spend the winter there are allowed to kill a limited number. As their numbers are still decreasing the time will soon come when the musk-ox in Greenland will also need to be given total protection.

The Arctic Wolf

AMONG THE animals the wolf is the only enemy of the musk-ox. Like the latter and the reindeer, it came to Greenland from Northern Canada, and was first recorded in North-east Greenland in 1899. The German expedition mentioned in the last chapter, which had wintered in the same region thirty years before, had seen no trace of wolves; one must therefore conclude that they were not then living in this area. Since 1899 they have frequently been seen by explorers and trappers. The area of distribution of the wolf is the same as that of the musk-ox, and it rarely leaves it, although their tracks have been seen on the south side of Scoresby Sound, and also a wolf has been shot in West Greenland, south of Melville Bay, near the Greenlandic colony of Umanak.

During winter in North-east Greenland wolf tracks are found on land, on the sea ice, and even on the Inland Ice, and one might think that they were abundant. I believe, however, that there are very few of them. In any case the wolf is certainly the rarest of the land mammals of Greenland, but it is always on the move, so that, within a short period of time, the same animal may be seen in two places quite far apart. They seem to live permanently in the wintering areas of the

musk-ox. Thus I have seen them in Hochstetter Foreland, Hudson
Land, Jameson Land, and Scoresby Land. Farther to the north they
are found round Danmark Fjord, and at the bottom of Independence
Fjord.

The Arctic wolf is white, and this is the only respect in which it
differs from the other greyish wolves. According to a report by the
naturalist Manniche, an adult male wolf killed on the Danmark Expedition, in Germania Land, measured 30 inches to the shoulder. The
length from the muzzle to the tip of the tail was 65 inches. A female
killed by the same expedition measured 33 inches to the shoulder and
63 inches in length. They were both in their white winter coats, but
one had a dark patch on the back and tail.

What does a Greenland wolf look like in summer? Nobody knows
exactly. I have seen them in summer, and they looked white with a
greyish back, but they were so far away that I could not be sure of the
colour. During their first summer coat the wolf cubs are completely
grey.

It is doubtful whether the wolves breed in Greenland, and it is
thought that all those seen there have come directly from Canada.
Nobody has yet found a lair or den or anything which suggests that a
wolf has remained in one place for any length of time. Wolf cubs, in
their first summer coats, have twice been seen, however, in Hurry
Inlet, near Scoresby Sound. In both cases it was a single cub accompanied by an adult, and they certainly could not have come from
Canada to Scoresby Sound, even over the Inland Ice. This shows that
the wolf can breed in Scoresby Sound, if only exceptionally, although
the majority of the Greenland wolves have probably first seen the light
of day in Canada.

Wolves wander about either alone or in pairs. They do not gather
in larger numbers—unless they are attracted during the winter by
depots of food, such as those established by expeditions and trappers.
For instance, one late evening in autumn, in Jameson Land, I saw four
wolves near a recently killed musk-ox. Their tracks in the new snow
showed that they had all come from different directions. When they

saw my companion and me approaching each went off its own way. During the whole of that autumn we found tracks of these four wolves in the eastern part of Jameson Land, but never saw two of them together. As soon as we had killed something, however, all four of them would congregate round the remains of the carcass. Again, in the following winter, three wolves prowled round our hut, each one coming from a different direction. We never saw them together, even when one of them had a fight with our sledge dogs. The same thing was observed by the Danmark Expedition when it wintered in Germania Land.

The wolf in Greenland lives under very hard conditions, caused not by the climate, but by the lack of food; this may account for its rarity and for the fact that it does not normally breed there. It has no particular prey, and of all Arctic animals it has the most varied diet. In its droppings I have found the remains of lemmings, hares, foxes, eggs, and birds, and I have often noticed that in spring it hunts young seals under the snow. On occasions it even attacks a musk-ox, but only, it seems, when the beast is old or ailing. Although a single wolf has no chance of killing a fit musk-ox, there is no doubt that they try. This is borne out by the large wounds found on most of the old wolves which are killed; these wounds have been made by the sharp horns of the musk-ox. In spring, however, they sometimes get hold of musk-ox calves at times when the adults are less vigilant. During the time when the calves are born I have often seen tracks in the snow, which showed that a wolf had been following a herd for some time, probably in the hope of attacking a newborn calf which had been allowed to stray from the parents. Sledge dogs often do this, so it would be still easier for a wolf, which is much stronger and faster.

During the long dark winter the wolf has to endure a period of famine. All the summer birds have disappeared, the lemmings are safely hidden away under the snow, and the musk-ox are gathered in large groups which can repulse any attacks. The only animal which it could hunt at this time is the hare, but it is a surprising thing that the wolf does not appear to be very clever at this. In the middle of winter

a wolf may wander across an area thick with hares, without making
the least effort to catch them. Dr A. L. V. Manniche has also found this
in the course of his studies on the wolf in Germania Land. I can give no
explanation for this behaviour. There is really little else the wolf can
eat, except carrion and the remains of fish and crustaceans occasionally
thrown up by the tide. It does, of course, make the most of any other
opportunities, and to a certain extent it competes with the less intelligent polar bear by digging for newborn seals out on the ice.

These varied food resources are too slender to nourish a great number of wolves, and, in fact, they enable only a few individuals to avoid
death from starvation.

Although the wolf is shy and distrustful towards man, it will sometimes approach him, especially in winter when hungry. During a
winter expedition in Scoresby Sound the wolves were such a nuisance
that we had to shut the sledge dogs in at night, to prevent the wolves,
which prowled all round the hut, from devouring them. The wolves
made off with anything that was edible. One day I had left the greater
part of a bear carcass on the ice near the shore, and above it had fixed
three heavy wolf traps. On the following day the whole lot had disappeared, and, as it had snowed in the meantime, there were no tracks
left. It was not until a month later that I found it on top of a block of
ice the height of a man, about half a mile out in the fjord. The scattered
bones round the traps showed that the wolves had dragged away the
whole of the carcass, which would have been much too heavy for a
man to carry.

The wolves were a particular nuisance to the Danmark Expedition,
which wintered at Danmarkshavn, on the south coast of Germania
Land. The report of Dr Manniche, the expedition's zoologist, says that
the wolves literally besieged the ship, which was held in the ice, and
the dogs could not be allowed out in the immediate vicinity. The
wolves did, nevertheless, succeed in killing four dogs and wounding
several others. When they attack a dog they always try to put it out of
action by wounding it in the head, before ripping open the belly.
Wolves also appeared during the sledge journeys on this expedition.

One of the explorers was attacked by three wolves while crossing Dove Bay, on his way back from Pustervig to the ship. In the twilight he thought it was a bear, and so released two dogs to give chase. One of them quickly returned to the sledge, trembling with fear, while the cries of the other showed that it was being attacked. On his approach one of the wolves fled, but the other two remained until shot at. Owing to the darkness, he missed them, and it was not until he examined the tracks that he realized that they were wolves. These animals followed his sledge for the remainder of the journey.

A month later another sledge was followed by two wolves, while on its way from the ship to Pustervig. They approached astonishingly close, but, owing to the darkness and bad weather, it was never possible to shoot them. In the evening there was a gale blowing, and so the travellers pitched their tent. The following morning, although the wind was still blowing hard, they heard pitiful howling from the dogs. One of the men, a Greenlander, took his gun and went out. He saw two wolves having a terrific fight with the dogs. One of them fled immediately, but the other remained, busily devouring a dog which it had killed. The Greenlander shot it from a distance of only a few feet. The wolf which had fled disappeared in the direction of the ship, and arrived there, some hours later, having run twenty-five miles.

There have been other incidents showing the aggressiveness of Arctic wolves. Dr Lauge Koch was travelling by sledge one spring from Scoresby Sound to Germania Land. With two of his travelling companions he stopped at the mouth of Dusen Fjord, on Ymer Island. This is his account of what happened:

> I had gone out that morning towards the mountain looking for fossils, but unarmed, as was my usual habit in North Greenland. As so often happens with us Arctic travellers, there may be one particular thing which really frightens us, and then we become as nervous as a woman faced by a mouse. If there is one thing that frightens me it is the track of a wolf, probably because it reminds me of the time, some ten years ago, when I lost one of my best friends, who was undoubtedly killed by a wolf; we never found any trace of him.

On the present occasion I saw an old wolf track, and this, added to a feeling that I was being followed, made me return to the tent faster than I had anticipated. Not far from the tent I saw that four wolves were following and gaining on me rapidly. Finally it became a race between the wolves and me. We all arrived together at the tent, where one of my companions killed one of them. The others fled towards the mountain.

This was the only dangerous incident we had on the journey. I should, however, have been experienced enough always to go out properly armed. It showed that, even if you are only leaving the tent for five or ten minutes, you should always take a gun with you.

The trappers also meet wolves. The Danish trapper Niels Hansen told me that, during the whole of one winter, his hunting area on Hochstetter Foreland was patrolled by a wolf, which upset his traps and stole sixteen foxes. After a number of unsuccessful attempts he finally caught it in a trap. It was an old she-wolf, with the hindquarters bearing a deep wound, and it had only half a tail. Niels Hansen gave me the skull. I have seen many skulls of old sledge dogs, which have more or less lost their teeth, but none were comparable with this one. There was, in fact, not a single complete tooth on the upper jaw, while there were no teeth at all on the lower jaw. The animal had been chewing directly on the jaw-bones, which showed deep markings as a result.

During the following year I was in the same area. After the first fall of snow in mid-October a solitary wolf was reported, at the bottom of Peter Bay, near to a Norwegian hunting-post. Three days later it was seen on the south coast of Hochstetter Foreland, near Cape Rink, where a Danish trapper tried to shoot it. From there it went over the ice to Kuhn Island. A week later its fresh tracks were found again

Page 63. *An Arctic fox eating the foot of a musk-ox.*
      An Arctic fox in its summer coat.
Page 64. *An Arctic fox hunting for lemmings.*
      The Arctic fox makes its lair in a dry place, often using a natural cavity among the boulders. On clear summer nights one not infrequently sees the cubs playing in front of the entrance to the lair.

near Cape Rink. It followed the coast northward, and then turned towards Shannon Island. Two days later it was back in Peter Bay, having come direct from Shannon Island, for its tracks were seen crossing Hochstetter Foreland. For three days it prowled around the low-lying area of Peter Bay, and then suddenly disappeared. It had run off north up to Bessel Fjord, where it was seen by Danish and Norwegian trappers. It remained there for forty-eight hours, turned south, and stayed for some time near Haystack, in Roseneath Bay. In three weeks it had travelled at least 190 miles. It had been seeking out the various places where musk-ox had been killed by the trappers, and this allowed me to keep a check on its movements.

Some trappers stationed in Roseneath Bay saw it in the darkness, eating meat stored near the tent for their dogs. They fired, but missed it. As it still remained in the area, they offered it some poisoned ptarmigan. The wolf sniffed at them, then urinated on them, but would not touch them. Then they put out some pieces of musk-ox, poisoned with strychnine. This was too tempting. The wolf ate them, and the following morning was found dead in the same place. It was not a particularly old wolf, and the teeth were healthy, with only one canine broken. The skin was pure white, and the animal was in good condition; it measured 61 inches from the muzzle to the tip of the tail and 26 inches to the shoulder. After its death no other wolf tracks were seen between Wollaston Foreland and Bessel Fjord. During this winter it must, in fact, have been the only wolf in an area the size of Jutland. This gives a good idea of how rare wolves are in North-east Greenland.

I have seen wolves at close quarters only on one occasion. This was during a sledge journey in spring, when I was in a fjord in the north-western part of Scoresby Sound. We had killed a musk-ox, and, while my two Greenlandic companions had gone to collect the meat, I

Page 65. *Polar-bear cubs, about four weeks old, playing in the snow.*
This young bear is looking for birds' nests and lemmings among the stones.
Page 66. *The abandoned den of a polar bear; the marks of their sharp claws are still visible.*
An adult male polar bear—master of the Arctic wastes.

remained in the tent. I had just gone out to fetch some snow to melt down when I was astonished to see three beautiful white dogs standing motionless a few yards from the tent. At first I did not think of wolves, but then I realized that we had no white dogs in our team. They seemed a little smaller than our sledge dogs, and much thinner. They appeared to be on the look-out and watched me with curiosity, but without showing the least surprise. I was on my knees in the entrance to the tent, and as long as I was there they stood completely still, like statues. Carefully I backed into the tent to get my camera and a gun, but when I returned to the entrance they had disappeared. Later we saw their tracks in the snow, and often heard them howling at night, but they never came so close again.

The wolf is usually so timid that it is seen only rarely. In general, it is an intelligent animal which makes the most of any opportunity of profit. It is entirely due to this that it has managed to survive in Arctic conditions, for which it is not particularly well adapted.

Arctic Hares

Hares are among the few land mammals that can adapt themselves to all climates, and so it is not surprising that one finds them in Greenland, where they are known as Arctic hares. These differ from the Scandinavian and Scottish hares by the stronger development of the hind-feet, and also because they remain white throughout the year. They have come here from the same areas and by the same route as the musk-ox, but their area of distribution in Greenland is not exactly the same, because they extend to the extreme south on the west coast. On the east coast, on the other hand, they scarcely reach farther south than the musk-ox—that is to say, not much farther down than Scoresby Sound. I am inclined to believe that in this case also it is the climate of this south-eastern area which discourages them. There is only one land mammal, the Arctic fox, which can live there, and even it is rare.

In the north-east there are so many hares that one can scarcely believe one's eyes. I have seen them in groups of a hundred at a time, and in some places one cannot walk for five minutes without seeing them. The hunters, who spend the whole year in the north-east of Greenland, estimate that the hare is increasing in numbers from year to year, as a result of the regular hunting of their natural enemy, the fox.

Arctic hares live on all kinds of terrain—on islands and steep rocks, along the coast, as well as on nunataks, which are the summits of mountains emerging from the Inland Ice. They dislike marshy ground and wide, flat plains, and prefer to live in the mountains during the winter. In summer they come down again towards the coast. In places where the mountains drop abruptly to the sea the hares may make pathways along the shore in the course of their nocturnal journeys from one grazing place to the next. At the approach of winter, as the low-lying regions become covered with snow, they move away from the coast and reach higher ground which the storms have swept free of snow. From this time until the beginning of spring they form groups of fifteen to twenty animals, sometimes more. These troops never remain close-packed, like those of the musk-ox. The hares seem to gather together quite at random in regions which are free of snow, and remain there as long as they can find food; then they disperse and join hares in other similar areas. They are the only land mammals in Greenland which do not seem to suffer from the harsh winter, and they find excellent shelter against the storms in crevices of rocks and under large boulders. When other animals are more or less famished, or living on the fat reserves which they have built up during the summer, the hares seem to be able to find plenty of nourishment.

In winter they leave the lower grounds, even though they are not always covered in snow. One finds them on the slopes from 300 feet above sea-level, and higher up their numbers increase with the altitude, even though vegetation there is very poor. Perhaps the explanation for this can be found in the observation made in the far north of Greenland by the Swedish botanist Wulf: "The frost attacks the plants very suddenly, and while they are still in full vigour. Not having the time to wither, they conserve the greater part of their nutritive elements in frozen form throughout the winter." This is also true in the east of Greenland, but only in the higher parts. This vegetation is so poor that it would be of no use to a large animal, such as the musk-ox, but is amply sufficient for the Arctic hare.

The hares gambol and graze all night, and then spend the day in the

shelter of a boulder, or in a rock crevice where they are shaded from
the sun. It is surprising to see how close one can get to a hare which,
counting on its camouflage and agility, does not feel the need to move
before danger becomes imminent. A whole troop can so dissimulate
themselves, on an apparently naked piece of ground, that at first sight
not a single one can be seen. I have found this on the Liverpool Coast,
and on the ill-famed Rathbone Island.

With two Greenlanders I was going up quite a steep slope when a
hare rose just in front of us. One shot killed it before it had disappeared.
With the detonation, hares appeared from all sides, as though a puff
of wind had brought innumerable tufts of white wool. The Greenlanders shot again, and when their cannonade ceased seven hares lay
dead. The others, about fifty of them, were sitting outside the range of
fire on top of the slope, watching us attentively. We continued our
march at the same height, and twenty minutes later the whole troop
had disappeared. As we passed the same spot on our return journey we
let off a shot into the air, and again hares appeared from all parts. By
the time we had reached the foot of the mountain their territory once
more had the appearance of a bare escarpment dotted with stones and
patches of snow; in fact, a landscape so deserted and abandoned that
one could scarcely believe it possible to find a single living creature.
This indicates how fruitful is the hunt for hares. Fur-hunters are
especially active at the beginning of winter, and thus are able to build
up a reserve of savoury game for the whole of the dark season.

The winter fur of the Arctic hare is relatively long and very soft, and
if it were only stronger it would certainly have the same value as that
of the fox. In addition it has the true whiteness of snow, unlike that of
the white Arctic fox, or of any other Arctic mammal. A hare sitting
on the snow, or near a patch of snow, is almost invisible. They blend
in with their surroundings so well that one can pass by a few feet away
without seeing them.

Mating starts at the end of April. The troops break up, couples are
formed, and each one takes up a small territory. They live in this way,
dispersed through the area in families, which remain independent of

one another right up to the autumn. After the mating season their long winter fur changes to a short summer coat. In this new dress the top of the nose, the forehead, and especially the front of the ears and a narrow stripe along the back are light grey, but at a distance they appear completely white.

While the Arctic hare belongs among those animals which resemble their surroundings, it may seem strange that those in Greenland retain, during the whole of the summer, a dress which differs so much from their surroundings. The dark summer coats of the fox, of the ermine, and of the lemming are not seen on the bare soil, while the hare can be made out from far away. When one is sailing in a fjord on one of the sunlit nights of summer one can see the hares innocently bounding about on the dark sides of the mountains without making the least effort to camouflage themselves. The contrast of these white hares with the snow-free earth is a typical phenomenon of the summer landscape in Greenland, and I have often heard it said that this contradicts the general opinion that the best protection of the hare against its enemies is the camouflaged nature of its fur. This is certainly true of the Arctic hares in other countries, but those of Greenland form an exception. The adults have no enemy to fear. The wolf, curiously enough, scarcely ever hunts them, while the small foxes of the mountains manage to catch them only accidentally; in fact, the hares can move much faster than either of these carnivores. Their agility protects them so well that camouflage would be of little use during the short Arctic summer. On the other hand, the leverets, which are much hunted by the fox, benefit by their perfect camouflage, for they have a grey fur which blends with the soil and the rocks.

Against man, who is undoubtedly their worst enemy, the confidence of the hares in their speed is completely misplaced, but they seem to find this difficult to understand. With enough patience and care one can approach very close to a hare and, into the bargain, even arouse its curiosity.

One day I wanted to take a close-up photograph of a hare crouching behind a large stone among the ruins of an Eskimo house, so I went up to it very slowly. Its only movement was to shift still closer against the stone and to put its head forward, so as to have a look at me. We were only about five yards apart. I remained motionless for a moment while it got used to my presence. Then I went up to the edge of the ruins, thus gaining two yards, and took my first picture. The noise of the shutter disturbed it a little, but it became calm again so soon that by the time I had taken a second picture it was quite used to me. I now had to find a way of dislodging it from behind the stone, because I could see only the head and part of the back. I started to whistle softly. Immediately it perked up an ear, then moved just enough for me to see its body, and sat down and watched me. Again I tried to attract it, but it still hesitated to approach me. Finally curiosity overtook its fear, and it left the stone and came towards the camera. I watched it grow bigger and bigger on the ground-glass screen of the camera until it filled the whole area. Suddenly something frightened it—I suppose a reflection from the lens—and, with a quick movement of the hind-legs, it bounded to one side and disappeared.

Towards the end of June, when the leverets are due to be born, the female seeks a patch of dry sand, preferably near to the slope where she has lived with the male during the mating season. There are usually seven in a litter, and they are all born grey. During the first two or three days they need all the attention of the mother, and she will not leave them in any circumstance, even when there is great danger, and will defend them valiantly against an enemy far superior in strength. After their third day the leverets are already able to protect themselves unaided against the numerous perils which surround them. When an enemy approaches, either a wandering fox or a wolf, they quickly slink away into hiding-places among the stones. They will do the same if a falcon, or a snowy owl, or a raven glides down on them and is then chased away by the mother. On several occasions whole litters of leverets have disappeared in front of me, as though by magic, and I have found it quite impossible to find more than two of them again, even though I have searched for more than an hour. Sometimes the leverets, when caught by surprise, gather close together one against the other with their heads in the centre, forming a rosette pattern, which so resembles a patch of pebbles that one is easily taken in by it.

In the north-east of Greenland the Arctic hares may, exceptionally, produce a number of litters in the year. Once in September in Manley Land, near Wordie Glacier, I killed a female which contained two completely formed fœtuses; the following year on Mount Muschel, in Hochstetter Foreland, I saw—again in September, and in two places— young leverets which could not have been more than three weeks old, but I consider these cases to be exceptional.

After the birth of the leverets the male regains his liberty. Sometimes he remains not far away from the place where the female is sheltering and feeding her young, but more often he abandons her completely. Only once have I seen a male help the female to defend her leverets against a fox.

The young very soon become independent. They leave the mother at an age of two to three weeks, when their coats turn from grey to white, but they still live together for some time. Often, at the beginning of autumn, a number of litters unite into groups composed entirely of leverets, but by the onset of winter they have become adult and mingle among their elders.

Page 75. *A polar bear during his endless wandering on the drift-ice.*
Page 76. *The tracks of a polar bear in the snow, showing clearly how it drags its feet with the paws just touching the snow.*

The Arctic Fox

THE ARCTIC fox is the only land mammal which is found through-out the whole of Greenland, and it is supposed to have come origin-ally from the extreme north of Canada. It is well able to adapt itself to the variations of the Arctic habitat and to overcome the difficulties of food and climate, which limit the distribution of other animals. Nevertheless, it is not equally abundant in all parts of the country. On both the west and east coasts there are certain areas which are particularly favourable for it. The country around Cape York and the mountains of the north-east, which have a big bird population, cer-tainly attract it, and so do some of the fjords—rich in fish—of the south-west. On the east coast it prefers the lemming country—that is, the northern half. It is not so abundant on the south-east coast, but it is found in the immediate neighbourhood of Scoresby Sound, where there are bird cliffs.

Arctic foxes may be either white or dark-coloured; the latter are known as blue foxes. In spite of this difference in colour, blue and white foxes belong to the same species, and there is no other difference between them. A white fox can mate with a blue fox and produce white or dark young. Mixing of the two colours does not occur, and two white animals may produce blue cubs, while a pair of blue foxes may have white offspring.

In North-east Greenland white foxes are by far the most numerous. Blue animals, which may be anything between steel blue and pale beige, are especially numerous near the bird cliffs on the Liverpool Coast, where half the captured foxes are blues, and around Dove Bay, where they form 30 per cent. of the population. Arctic trappers are well aware that, in general, the greatest number of blue foxes is found near the bird cliffs. It is very characteristic that only blue foxes are found on the small islands of the Arctic Ocean, which are really just bird cliffs isolated in the sea. This is probably due to the fact that the birds live on cliffs and rocks, which are steep and dark in colour, and where the snow does not lie in winter. In such places the fox population has evolved a darker protective colouration than on the snow-clad areas, where nearly all the foxes are white.

The proportion of blue and white foxes on snow-free and snow-clad areas is very constant, and, if one knows the physical appearance of the terrain and the food resources, one can easily estimate the percentage of blue foxes in a given area.

In summer the short-haired fur of the white foxes becomes dark. Their backs are greyish or brownish with a few scattered white hairs, and the belly is yellowish. They may also have large dark or light patches spread over the whole body. At this period the difference between white and blue foxes is so slight that they are often difficult to distinguish. Compared with the foxes of other Arctic countries and of Scandinavia, those in Greenland are generally smaller. The dimensions of the Greenland specimens may vary considerably, and quite independently of sex and age. Those from mountain country are nearly always small and light in build; their fur is very fine and therefore much prized.

The difficulties of existing at all in the severe winters of North-east Greenland cause the fox to keep on the move the whole time. It prefers to remain near the coast, where it searches the driftline for small fish, seaweed, crustaceans, and other debris thrown up by the sea. But this in no way serves to satisfy its hunger, and it would be no better off than the wolf if it did not lay up a store of game during the summer season. It is especially birds, birds' eggs, and lemmings that it carefully hides away in a rock crevice or under a big boulder, covering them all up with gravel and sand. The larder is sited in a place which is shaded from the sun; otherwise the heat would quickly generate a smell and attract other animals.

One only rarely finds these caches, for they are always put in spots where they are soon covered by snow; so they are not discovered until the fox has opened them up, and then they are empty. I only once managed to find one intact. The fox had quite recently come and dug it up, but something or other must have frightened it away. This larder was hidden in a rock crevice, and covered with about eighteen inches of snow. It contained thirty-six little auks, two young guillemots, and four snow-buntings, as well as a large number of little auk eggs. The frozen bodies of the birds were neatly arranged in a long row at the foot of the crevice, and the eggs were heaped in a pile up against the rock-face. The whole store would have provided food for a fox for at least a month, particularly if it could find some additional food outside. As each fox makes a number of these caches, one can well understand how they manage to get through the bad season without suffering from hunger, while even in normal winter conditions the wolves go hungry.

In the first days of spring, when the polar bear starts to hunt seals on the fjord ice and along the coasts, the fox follows on its tracks to eat up the remains of the kill. Sometimes the excrement of the bear contains incompletely digested material on which the fox will feed: but he himself can also hunt seals, for his sense of smell enables him to find the newborn young when they are hidden away under the snow.

In general, the beginning of spring sees the fox living almost the whole time out on the sea ice and often far from the coast. When the ice starts to break up, the piece on which he is being carried may drift off from the firm ice, so that he cannot get back to land. Foxes have been seen on drift-ice ninety miles from land. They were all starving and came right up to the ships, in some cases jumping aboard to search for offal and scraps.

Arctic foxes start to mate during the first fortnight of March. The trappers say that from this time until the beginning of April very few foxes are caught, because they are all so busy seeking each other that they are quite unattracted by the bait in the traps.

During the early days of May each pair settles down in its own territory and lives in a lair, which is either dug by them in the earth or which may be just a natural hole. The vixen has her young at the end of May or at the beginning of June. She may have up to twelve cubs, but she does not rear them all unless she herself is well nourished—that is, when lemmings are abundant. She also eats leverets and young birds, but lemmings are the basic diet, to such an extent that the foxes are always more numerous in what are known as good lemming years. When food is scarce many of the cubs are condemned to die from hunger. It also seems that the vixen may kill and eat them all when she is unable to rear them. It is only the foxes which live near the bird cliffs that are independent of the lemmings, and their numbers scarcely vary from one year to the next.

Most of the explorers who worked in Greenland before fox-trapping began considered the animal as an amusing guest around the winter camps, and a faithful companion on sledge journeys, although at the same time it could be a bit of a rascal. Lieutenant Payer, a member of the Second German Polar Expedition to Greenland, gives the following amusing account of the fox's behaviour:

> The European fox avoids man; the Greenland one, on the other hand, innocently and confidently seeks his company, for it hopes above all to profit by it. After a successful hunt it is the first to express admiration for the hunter and to claim a share in the booty. It will accompany him on his sledge journeys—at a respectful distance—and profit from his slumbers

to open and pillage his food stores. It takes kindly to a ship imprisoned in the ice, for from her will come all sorts of unusable scraps which are easy to steal. It is so accustomed to the rôle of parasite that it is often difficult to protect it from its own cheekiness.

If one leaves the tent to get it to stop making a noise, or, if there are many of them, their surly yelping, instead of just slipping off, they will stand and impudently watch their benefactor. If one lets off a shot they move off slowly and with bad grace. At other times the fox will approach from curiosity, without any show of fear, even if one shoots at it, and if it finds a piece of meat it will follow the tracks of a sledge for miles.

During my first winter at Scoresby Sound I also found that the fox was an amusing, if importunate, hanger-on. There were six of us living in a wooden hut left by a previous expedition. We had been there for about fifteen days when we noticed that a pile of jam-tins and other rubbish near the hut had been visited during the night. The following day we found the tracks of foxes in the snow, and they were not long in showing themselves. At first there were only a few of them—as far as I remember two blue foxes and one white one—who warily approached our home at dusk. They were still mistrustful and would not let us come close to them, so we all agreed to leave them alone; they had the right to live near us if it so pleased them, and we had no dogs to chase them away. The results of this policy were quite unexpected. Some days later there were more of them, and one evening we counted twenty-two.

All night long these much-prized fur animals rummaged around in the heap of rubbish, most of which consisted of damaged tins which we had thrown out. When the foxes saw us during the day they would let us approach only to a distance which still allowed them to escape if necessary—until one of us had the idea of feeding them. It seemed as though the foxes had been waiting for this. Their behaviour changed completely. Now it was they who approached us, and we did nothing to prevent them. As soon as one had dared to take the offered piece of meat, the whole company ran towards the hut. We had to be careful that, in their haste to outdo their companions, these foxes did not seize our hands as well as the proffered scraps. The first autumnal gales were starting at about this time. It often blew for several days on end, and there was a lot of snow. As long as the storm was raging no fox was visible, but afterwards they would return in even larger numbers. So as to have more control of our new neighbours we took to feeding them from the window, where they would come one by one to take their pieces of meat from a fork. The front of our window soon became a snack-bar for all the foxes in the neighbourhood. Most of them never left the vicinity, and made holes in the snow or among the boulders, where they spent the day.

Unfortunately the company of these foxes made life quite intolerable. Scarcely a night passed without such brawling round the hut that one of us had to get up and throw them something to eat before we could get any sleep. We took it all in good spirit, and were so happy to see these beautiful animals and so pleased to have their confidence that nobody thought of harming them—until one fine day when things went wrong. We had been out hunting in the mountains. When we returned to the hut late in the evening it was swarming with foxes. They were in the beds and underneath them, on the cooking stove and in the saucepans, and some had even crept into our sleeping-bags and soiled them. All the available food had been devoured or rendered useless.

A short time afterwards we left this hut and returned to the head-quarters of the expedition. The foxes followed us to the shore, and watched with interest as we embarked. I set free a little white fox which I had in captivity, and immediately he joined the others, without showing the least desire to run away.

One day later on, when the fjord was frozen over, we saw the whole troupe of foxes arriving. Many of them we could recognize—especially one blue fox who had been wounded and lost a front paw. Their numbers were still large, but the days of friendship were over. Their rich winter pelts had grown again, and we started to hunt them, and so the charm was broken.

The Polar Bear

THE POLAR bear forms a kind of transition between the land mammals and the marine mammals of the High North. It lives permanently on the east coast of Greenland, and appears as a visitor only on the west coast. Its true habitat is around the drift-ice along the coast, where it is attracted by the seals, and it also occurs as far out as the edge of the pack-ice.

The migrations of polar bears on the drift-ice are determined by those of the seals. During winter, when the seals live under the ice along the coast and in the fjords, the bears have almost completely deserted the shore. They then live far out along the edges of the big patches of open water which appear in the ice, and off the outermost islands such as Sabine, Shannon, and Great Koldewey. Only there can they capture the young seals which are not yet capable of maintaining breathing-holes in the ice. They also spend the winter at the mouth of the vast Scoresby Sound, where there is often some open water. They do not return from the drift-ice to the coast until the end of the Arctic night—that is, from about mid-February to mid-March.

By then ringed seals have had their young under the snow, which is still lying on the ice, and the bears move to places where such game is abundant, particularly Scoresby Sound and its numerous ramifications. In no other part have I observed such a marked migration of bears. One year between February 23 and 29 twenty-one bears entered the fjord, and the Greenlanders killed twelve of them, of which eleven were old males. The Greenlanders consider that it is always the old males which start the spring migration. This attains its peak in the first half of March. During a sledge journey from Scoresby Sound to Cape Dalton which I once made in spring, we met fifty-two bears in three days between our point of departure and Henry Land, and among them were many females with young of quite a good size. This migration stopped about the middle of March as suddenly as it had begun.

The bears also frequent Dove Bay, which has natural conditions rather similar to those of Scoresby Sound, notably in that it produces many icebergs which have a strong influence on the presence and reproduction of the seals. Bears go there regularly every spring and seek out these breeding-places among the icebergs.

The duration of the bears' stay on the coast is very variable. They hunt newborn seals for about a month, at the latest up to the middle of May, and then they return to the drift-ice. This new migration goes on up to the autumn, when the sea freezes over again. It is much slower than the spring migration, because from time to time the bears wander to the mainland, where they eat blueberries and grass.

By the early days of autumn most of the bears are back on the drift-ice, hunting the larger species of seals, and especially their young. In this way they travel south, and every autumn the Greenlanders of Angmagssalik expect a regular influx of bears, of which they take their toll.

The bears wander about on the ice all through the winter, and then turn back northward again to reach Scoresby Sound and the other large fjords in the spring, tempted again by a diet of baby seals. The females do not take part in these migrations when they are pregnant

Page 87. *A collared lemming.*
Page 88. *An ermine in its winter coat.*

or when they are feeding the young, nor during the following year, as they are then accompanied by their cubs. I will deal with this subject in more detail a little later.

The movement of drift-ice from the polar basin towards Greenland is constantly bringing other polar bears from the north of Spitsbergen and from Franz Josef Land, where they are still abundant. There are even some far to the north of these two archipelagos. On this point the Norwegian explorer Fridtjof Nansen has written:

> In the interior of the polar sea he [the bear] is not very common because he does not find much food there; I have, however, seen the tracks of a bear north of 83° N., and near the *Fram*, in 1896, a bear was killed at 84° N., 26° E. Presumably the bear is able to wander across the whole of the Arctic Ocean even up to the Pole itself.

The polar bear is the largest and strongest of all bears still surviving. The biggest males of which I have records measured 7 feet 11 inches from the muzzle to the tip of the tail, of which 8 inches were tail. The females are a little smaller; among the 23 which I have measured none were longer than 6 feet 1 inch, but they can reach a length of 6½ feet.

The fur is yellowish, the nose black, and the eyes dark brown. In silhouette the polar bear is characterized by having the hindquarters rather higher than the front-quarters. This, together with the long and powerful neck and the small head, makes it easily recognizable as a good swimmer. On the ice and on land its movements seem heavy and clumsy—an impression which is strengthened by the fact that it walks with an ambling gait—but, being possessed of enormous power, it is able when necessary to be astonishingly swift and light-footed. I have seen bears moving so fast on the fresh-polished ice that no dog could catch them, and they are absolutely unequalled in deep snow, where, with their long limbs and great paws, they can move faster than any

Page 89. *A complete family of walruses with young. In the foreground is an old female, easily recognizable by the divergence of the tusks.*
Page 90. *Four old walruses resting on the sand near some rocks. At one time the fine tusks of the walrus were much prized.*

other animal. They are clever climbers, and when hunted they can get up the steepest icebergs, where no dog can follow. On the mainland their tracks have been found up to heights of 3000 feet.

The seal is its favourite food, but, being omnivorous, the polar bear also eats carrion and is not averse to eating the remains of one of its own companions. Its stomach is often found to contain grass and berries, and the Greenlanders believe that it also eats seaweed, and if it comes across a colony of eider-ducks during the breeding season it will plunder all the nests. It can even catch the quick-moving lemmings by turning over the stones under which they are hiding. Fridtjof Nansen found the skin and blubber of a young white whale in the stomach of a bear which he had killed. According to the Norwegian explorer, the bear can catch small whales by jumping down on them from the edge of the ice or from the shore where it is keeping watch. On the other hand, it respects the walrus. No one has ever seen a polar bear attack a walrus, either on the ice or in the water. I have seen a bear come close up to a walrus, on an ice-floe, without the two animals paying the slightest attention to each other, and Nansen observed the same thing in Franz Josef Land. The walrus paid no attention to the polar bear even when the latter passed quite close to it. Presumably the walrus is too strong and too dangerous for the bear to risk an attack. Also, in the water, the walrus is far superior to the bear, and, spiteful as he is towards all animals in his vicinity, he often makes the bear flee. Besides, the bear is defenceless in the water. I have seen a bear chased by a group of young ringed seals, which swam up against it and tried to bite its hindquarters. The bear rounded on them many times, but none the less hastened to gain the nearest ice-floe.

In the stomach of a bear which was killed in Scoresby Sound I have found pieces of meat and skin of musk-ox, and not far away the carcass of the beast on which it had feasted. The trapper Andersen told me that, in his hunting reserve on Kuhn Island, he once found the tracks of a musk-ox and a bear so intermingled that there had undoubtedly been a fight between these two animals, but the tracks separated out without showing the result. On the other hand, during the winter of

1932, at Walrus Point, in Germania Land, the trapper Jensen found a musk-ox which had shortly before been killed by a bear. He had himself seen the bear while making the round of his traps. On his return he followed the tracks of the beast and came across a dead ox, still warm and showing marks which proved how it had been killed. All around the snow was trampled and bespattered with blood. With its claws the bear had badly lacerated the head of its victim, had torn off and thrown to a distance of several yards some large pieces of skin, and had eaten half the hindquarters. Judging from the tracks in the snow, it must have been a large male bear, and it did not appear to have been wounded in the fight. I do not consider it impossible that a bear could overcome a musk-ox enfeebled by age, or a young one isolated from the herd, but this is certainly a rare occurrence. I do not, however, believe that a bear has the least chance against a herd, or even against a solitary musk-ox in full prime, whose horns are redoubtable weapons.

The bear is a master in the art of killing seals. He uses the most astute methods to glide up towards the prey, and then suddenly to bound forward and deliver the mortal blow. As I have said, he is unable to catch them in the water, and it is only on the ice that he kills them. As silent as a cat, he creeps towards the seal, hiding behind irregularities on the ice. If the seal lifts its head he immediately flattens himself out and becomes motionless. It has been said that he uses one paw to hide the black tip of his muzzle so that it will not betray him! As soon as the seal has assured itself that all is well the bear advances again until he can jump on to it and kill it with a blow on the head.

When the ice is flat and lacking in hiding-places the bear moves along on his belly, and, according to the Greenlanders, pushes a piece of ice in front of him as cover!

One day, at the mouth of Scoresby Sound, I saw a bear capture its prey. A young ringed seal, about half-grown, was basking in the sun at the edge of a small ice-floe. The bear had seen it from the edge of the fast ice. He stood up for a moment to scent the air and to examine the position of the seal, and then he entered the water in a rather strange way. Approaching the water's edge backward, he gripped the ice with his front paws, and then put first one hind-leg then the other into the water. Finally, he let go his grip on the ice, and let himself sink until only his muzzle remained above the surface. This seemed a very clumsy method, but he succeeded in this way in getting into the sea with the least noise. I was about seventy yards from the place, and with powerful glasses was able to observe every movement of the hunter. He swam towards the seal with the tip of his nose making only a very slight ripple on the surface of the water. When he was ten yards from the ice-floe he lifted his head cautiously, just enough for me to see his ears, and then dived. Suddenly the thin skin of ice which had formed round the floe shattered into pieces, and the head of the bear appeared exactly underneath the seal, which was completely taken by surprise. Before it could make the slightest movement the bear brought his paw on to its head and killed it with a single stroke.

Fridtjof Nansen tells how, near Jan Mayen Island, in the Arctic Ocean between Greenland and Spitsbergen, the bear will play with the young seals lying out on the ice, like a cat with a mouse: "He takes the seal in his paw and throws it high into the air, rolls it like a ball, then leaves it half-dead, to start the game again with another one."

Polar bears mate in the second half of April, and this is the only period when one can see the two adults together. The males are very aggressive at this time, and when they meet there is always a bloody fight. I have had many pelts of male bears in my hands, and they all, without exception, showed wounds on the hindquarters.

A large bear may prove very dangerous to its less powerful companions, and this is well shown by the following incident which Nansen witnessed during his stay in Franz Josef Land in the spring of 1895, and which he describes in his book *Among Seals and Bears*.

> One night we had a visit from a large male bear which was exceptionally thin—he had not a trace of fat, either under the skin or in the stomach. Extremely emaciated, he had come to our reserve of fat, which was on a hillock. We had recently killed a female bear which had two cubs already quite large. They had run off, but remained in the neighbourhood of our hut. The following night they came back and devoured the belly and

entrails of their mother. Perhaps they had also gone close to our reserve of fat when the large male arrived. From the tracks we saw that he had followed one of them, and killed it a little farther away on the pack-ice, then he had pursued the other one and had killed it too. Finally, he must have come back to our fat reserve, eaten his fill, and then fallen asleep on the spot. We found him there when we left our hut in the morning.

The female polar bear has her young at the end of January or the beginning of February. She makes a hole in the snow along the shore. This den differs in form from that made in winter by the male, either as a shelter against snowstorms or as a place in which to digest a good meal. It is a real home, consisting of an entrance passage, about twenty-seven inches high and nine feet long, leading into a spacious chamber. When it is first constructed the entrance passage is very short, and only attains its full length in spring, when the animal leaves the den. Its length depends mainly on the quantity of snow which has accumulated on top of the shelter in the course of the winter. At the end of the corridor there is generally a sort of separation wall between the vestibule and the chamber.

The bear cubs are born astonishingly small—scarcely the size of a guinea-pig—and are completely blind for the first two weeks. They live for a good month in the den, and during this time their mother never leaves them, and so she never gets any food. The case, cited in the chapter on musk-ox, when a female bear left her young for a moment seems to me exceptional, as was the reason for her curiosity. The litter may consist of two cubs, but often there is only a single one. In their expressive language the Greenlanders affirm that one can go the whole lifetime of a man without seeing a female polar bear with three cubs.

Towards the end of their stay in the den the bears seem to play and exercise themselves in turn. The elevation at the end of the entrance corridor serves as a practice ground for climbing. In abandoned dens I have often found traces of their little claws, and here and there they have dug holes. On a fine day at the beginning of March or April the mother leads her offspring into the open air. It seems that the females with a single cub leave their dens first, while those which have two cubs to rear do not leave until about a month later. By then the young are as large as a fox, but they are quick enough to follow the mother without apparent difficulty, although she does not let them get tired. Generally they do not go far away from the den for some days, and they still spend the nights in it. During the day they make little expeditions in the neighbourhood. The nearest snowy slope serves as a slide, and the mother makes them try their strength by getting them to climb a ramp, whence they redescend by sliding on their bellies—a game which they obviously enjoy. One day I surprised a family of bears in the middle of such a game. The mother stood down at the bottom of the slope, catching the infant gambollers with her front paws each time they arrived at the bottom, happily growling and completely covered in snow.

As they are unable to make long journeys with their young, the females spend the succeeding winter in the interior of the fjords, and also remain there during the second winter. By the following spring the cubs have developed their second dentition and are the size of a large sledge dog, but they are still being suckled by the mother. Nevertheless, their stay in the fjords has come to an end, and in the course of the summer the female leads them out on to the drift-ice. According to the Greenlanders, who are excellent observers, the cubs receive lessons in hunting seals. When the mother advances towards the prey the little ones follow immediately at her tail and imitate all her movements, right up to the moment when she throws herself on the seal, The hunting lessons take place partly in the water, where the young have to follow her. Later on she allows the cubs to practise on their own, while she remains near by.

In the following year the young bears are as large as their mother; the young males are even a little larger, and so easily recognizable. Their movements, however, still appear clumsy and infantile. The mother usually leaves them at this time, because once more she is in season, and this separation takes place immediately before, if not at the moment of, mating. Nevertheless, in autumn one can sometimes see a female still followed by large young bears, but I am not sure whether, in such cases, she has already started a new pregnancy. After they have left their mother the young ones remain together for a short time, and then each goes its own way.

The descriptions of the old seal-hunting expeditions in the Arctic Ocean often mentioned formidable hunts for polar bears, in which the animals are described as frightful monsters. There is one particularly gruesome story of a fight between the crew of a ship and a gigantic bear. As the Arctic fauna became better known, the descriptions of hunts became less dramatic. Little by little the bear returned to its true size, and some travellers even came to the point of suggesting that it was completely inoffensive. In actual fact it can attack and kill a man.

A member of the East Greenland Hunting Company had gone out on to the pack-ice to paint—or so they say—and not having returned by the evening, his companions went to search for him. They found him lying in the snow with a smashed skull. The surrounding tracks showed that he had been killed by a bear, but naturally we do not know exactly what happened. Probably the bear was attracted by curiosity, and the man did not see it until it was right on top of him. He must have tried to defend himself when he was attacked by the frightened animal, for his gun was found open with a cartridge in the barrel. It is also possible that the bear was hungry, but, whatever happened, it did not eat its prey. This striking case shows that it is not always sufficient to be armed; one must also be constantly on the look-out.

Of all the expeditions to the north-east of Greenland, the first which wintered in the country was the one most troubled by the polar bear; at this time the animal appears to have been more numerous than it is to-day. There were two occasions on which a man was nearly killed, both quite near to the winter quarters of the expedition in Germania Port (Sabine Island). In one case it was a miracle that the man escaped.

On the first occasion a sailor went out unarmed, and so at his own risk and peril, for a walk on Mount Germania. He was resting at the summit when he suddenly saw a large bear standing some feet away from him. The man fled precipitously. Turning round while he was running, he saw that the bear was pursuing him and gaining ground. His cries did not frighten the beast, but seemed, on the contrary, only to stimulate it. In order to distract the attention of the animal the sailor threw off his jacket. The bear examined it, and then resumed the chase faster than before. The sailor again threw off pieces of his clothing. Each one served to slow down the bear for a moment, but not enough to prevent its relentless approach. The bear was soon so close that the man gave up and remained rooted to the spot. He could feel the cold muzzle of the bear sniffing at his hands. In the meantime his companions had heard his cries and were rapidly approaching. The bear saw them and moved away from the sailor as though to take stock of the situation. For a moment it remained indecisive, and then ran off.

Another time, late at night, one of the scientists of the expedition, Dr Börgen, had gone ashore to make some astronomical observations. On his return, at some fifty yards from the ship, which was firmly held in the ice, he was attacked by a bear. He himself wrote later: "The attack was so sudden that I cannot now say whether the bear stood up and hit me with his paw, or whether he knocked me over as he ran by."

Dr Börgen had no time to use his gun. The bear bit his head so severely that he could hear its teeth grinding against his skull. His cry frightened the bear, which let go for a moment and then started to bite him again. The crew of the ship ran up shouting, but this only incited the bear to run off with its prey, which it still held firmly by the head. A shot made it let go, but then it seized him by the arm, although this time less securely. Then, gripping the doctor's right hand, it dragged him along the shore over the pack-ice. The roughness of

Page 99. *Disturbed from their slumbers, these walruses are about to slide into the water.*

Page 100. *A ringed seal, with head out of water, has a look round.*

A recently killed bearded seal. In life the bristly moustache is held off the ground.

the ice made the bear slacken speed, and finally it left its victim so as to escape more easily.

Usually a polar bear approaches man out of pure curiosity. This is especially the case with the males, who, aware of their superior strength, are quite fearless, and who at the same time must always investigate anything unusual in their surroundings. Food depots left on the coast by expeditions or by fur-trappers are particularly subject to this inquisitiveness. Even when these are constructed with large boulders the bear always manages to ransack them. He tears open the tins with his teeth, eats what he can, and spreads the remainder over a large area. He amuses himself by rolling on to the pack-ice anything he can move, such as large tins and barrels. I have seen one pushing along a petrol-can on the ice, and the Danish hunter Christoffersen has told me that, near to one of his huts, a bear had moved a large barrel full of milk on to the pack-ice, and abandoned it there in a battered condition.

When a male bear sees a man, whether on land or on the ice, its insatiable curiosity always makes it approach. It comes along in its usual amble, without any sign of hurrying, and there is no means of getting out of its way. Every movement or noise excites its curiosity. There's nothing else to do but to shoot. If one is unarmed and without shelter it seems to me that the best plan is to remain quite still, for it does not necessarily follow that the bear will do you any harm when it does eventually reach you; it may lose interest before it gets to you, or only sniff at you and then move off. I can vouch for this, because I once found myself unarmed in the presence of a bear in the following circumstances. The terrain was unsuitable for the sledges, and so I had gone on ahead on skis to find a route, and, thinking I would soon return, I had left my gun on the sledge. I had reached the foot of a glacier and was looking for a route when, suddenly, I saw a bear. It

Page 101. *Eskimos in their frail kayaks hunting in a fjord still full of ice.*
Page 102. *A female ptarmigan in winter plumage. In the male the black line joins the eye to the beak.*
A female ptarmigan in summer plumage.

did not appear to have seen me, and so I immediately tried to hide between two blocks of ice at the foot of the steep wall of the glacier. To do this I had to remove my skis; I sank in up to my knees in the snow and was quite immobilized. The bear was ambling along quite peacefully, and it still did not appear to have noticed me. When it reached the tracks made by my skis it stopped and sniffed the air. Then for a moment it gazed far away on to the ice. It turned its head and at the same time saw me. The distance between us was exactly five paces. I did not move a muscle. The bear remained watching me for about a minute. I was still quite motionless, but I swear I could hear my heart beating. Then the animal moved off and continued its journey as though I did not exist. I have no doubt that if I had moved at the critical moment, or shouted for help, it would have come at me and the situation would have been very tricky.

I have, however, also seen a bear run away frightened when it found itself face to face with a man. It was a young bear which had strayed close to a trapper's hut where I was staying with a companion. Not suspecting that we were there, the bear came in by the door, which was half-open. It took such fright when we moved to find a gun that at first it was quite petrified. Then it tried to rear up, but was prevented by the frame of the door. It watched us, obviously not daring to come any closer, moved its head to one side, but was unable to turn round. Then it gave a groan, retreated backward, and fled so fast towards the beach that we were only just able to see it plunge into the sea.

The female bear, whether alone or accompanied by small or grown cubs, always tries to escape from man, and the young of either sex do the same. To a certain degree they all like to examine anything unusual, but they are terrified by man. In any case they will only rarely approach as close as the adult males.

When wounded most bears try to run away. I have never seen a wounded bear attack; they immediately try to get away from the hunter. They will, however, charge if there is no means of escape.

The polar bear is the most noble game in Greenland. Even the most

sophisticated hunter will not shrink from a difficult journey across the
ice to try his luck against the sovereign of the polar world. Nevertheless,
when one has lived in North-east Greenland for several years it is
difficult to understand the reason for this. To kill a bear can be considered neither as an exploit which enhances the status of the hunter
nor as a sporting performance worthy of the art of hunting. In every
case there is too much brutality in it to give pleasure. I have always
hated to see this magnificent beast rolling in its own blood on the ice,
and biting itself where the shot has penetrated, without attempting in
any way to use its enormous strength against the attacker. It is bad
enough to have to kill it when one is forced to.

For the Eskimos polar-bear hunting is quite a different thing. This
is for them a traditional job, and the only means which makes it possible
for them to live in the country at all. The superiority of the East
Greenlanders is seen in the way they do it. The man who first sights the
bear becomes the owner of the skin, whether the animal is killed by
him or by another, and he who kills a bear first sighted by another can
claim only a part of the meat. The following incident shows how well
this system of sharing is respected. One morning, when leaving home,
a girl of twelve years sees a bear on the ice. As her father is away she
raises the alarm among the neighbours. A hunter leaves immediately
with his sledge and kills the bear. Before dusk he has already delivered
the skin and a part of the meat to the little girl, who naturally passes
it all to her parents.

The Greenlanders of Scoresby Sound hunt the polar bear throughout the year, but especially on the ice in spring. Their sledge dogs serve
as a pack of hounds; they surround the bear, preventing it from escaping, until the hunters arrive to kill it. One cannot deny that hunting
done in this way may be exciting and even dangerous. When it takes
place on rough ice the sledge is jolted from one block to the next,
while the Greenlanders have the greatest difficulty in retaining control
of their dogs. In their eagerness the dogs are insensible to all cries, and
even to the whip, as they rush forward like madmen in pursuit of the
bear. At the right moment the hunter releases two or three of his best

dogs to overtake and stop the bear. The dogs usually attack the bear from the rear and bite it in the hindquarters. Even if they cannot wound it they make it sit down in order to protect this part of its body against their sharp teeth. This gives the hunter time to arrive with the main pack and get within shooting distance, and it is then easy for him to make the kill.

The bear, however, does not always allow the dogs to stop him so easily. If possible he gallops towards an iceberg or a steep rock, and climbs up to the top where the dogs cannot follow him. This makes no difference, however, to a hunter who has a weapon with a good range.

When the sea-ice is new and thin the bear has an ingenious method of throwing off its pursuers. It simply breaks the ice beneath it. It does this by jumping up and letting its whole weight come down on the ice, which shatters into pieces. The cracks can spread out so far that the hunter and his dogs may be in danger of drowning. The bear then plunges in and swims for a short time under the ice, but cannot go far from the hole, to which he has to return for breathing. This allows the Greenlander to get a shot at it, but he has little chance of actually reaching the bear across the thin ice, and so he usually abandons the hunt.

A polar-bear hunt as carried out nowadays by the Greenlanders usually presents little danger or difficulty, but in the days before the use of firearms, which is only about a man's lifetime ago, a hunt must have been really exciting. When the dogs had halted the bear, the hunter had to approach to within a few paces, and choose the right moment to plunge a harpoon into its breast—a particularly dangerous procedure.

It is easy to hunt a bear in the water. It does not swim so fast that one cannot catch it up in a rowing-boat, and it does not attempt any kind of defence. A Greenlander, however, always tries to avoid killing a bear in the water, because a single man cannot haul the body up on to the ice or on to land. A bear floats so deep in the water that only a thin fringe of hairs emerges from the surface. Besides, it is easy for the hunter to direct the living bear towards the point where he wants to kill it. The bear swims steadily in front of the bow of the kayak, and if it starts to drift to one side or the other a signal with the paddle suffices to bring it back on course. When it hauls itself out of the water at the chosen spot the hunter can quickly make the kill.

Polar-bear meat is very tasty, and is appreciated by Europeans wintering in Greenland as well as by the Eskimos. The liver, however, contains a toxin which makes it inedible. On the Danmark Expedition an investigation was carried out into effects of eating bear liver. The Expedition's doctor, I. Lindhard, reported that:

> ... nineteen men took part in the meal, and all of them became ill. The sickness manifested itself in the form of sleepiness, general malaise, and headaches. In general the symptoms could be described as a kind of intoxication similar to that caused by eating fresh shark meat. Afterwards the skin started to peel, in some cases only on the head, in others over the whole body.

Polar-bear skins are commercially valuable to the Greenlanders on the east coast. The summer pelts are less valuable than those of winter, because they lack the woolly down and the outer hairs are shorter. The pelts of adult males can be recognized by the short, tight hairs on the back. The fur of the females and of the young bears is generally longer and less yellow than that of the males. Bears which have lived principally on the pack-ice have sharp, pointed claws, while those which have been on land for a long time have claws which are worn and blunt.

The Lemming and the Ermine

THE COLLARED lemming of Greenland is a little smaller than the lemming of Scandinavia; it is about the size of a large fieldmouse, and when young it is similarly coloured. The adult lemming, however, has soft, compact, and silky fur, and its dark-grey back is, so to speak, framed from head to tail by a glistening red-brown border. This band is extended on each side of the neck to form a collar, whence the name for this particular kind of lemming. The belly is whitish with a pale-reddish tint. Towards the end of autumn the beautiful red-brown bands disappear, and give place to white fur, which extends progressively from the belly to the back. By the beginning of winter, when the ground is covered in snow, the lemming is clothed in a long white fur which protects it against the white background just as well as its dark summer coat did against the naked earth.

Being a rodent, the lemming is principally vegetarian, and the delicate new leaves of the Arctic willow are its favourite food. It also likes the roots of certain grasses, which it digs up easily with its strong claws; but in winter it has to eat almost any kind of vegetable matter. I have several times confirmed that it will eat flesh. The first occasion was on the frozen sea-ice, where a lemming was quietly gnawing away at a piece of seal meat which had been thrown out from my tent. This gave me the idea of feeding meat to a number of lemmings that I was keeping in captivity. They ate it with apparent satisfaction, without differentiating between the flesh of birds and mammals, but they would not touch the fat. I suppose that in the wild they do, on occasion, eat carrion and even small birds. Another characteristic feature of this little animal is that, like the polar bear, it ambles along.

The lemming spends the greater part of its life underground. It builds itself a burrow beneath the earth, which shelters it against storms and protects it from the frost. This burrow has a main entrance and two or three secondary ones. The entrance, which is only just large enough for it to crawl through, is four to six feet long, and it leads to a chamber about the size of a clenched fist, in which the animal makes a warm nest of dry grass. The other accessory entry channels are used only as lavatories. Their size determines the length of time during which the lemming will occupy its burrow, for as soon as they are full the animal has to abandon the burrow and dig another one elsewhere. In areas where the lemming is abundant the earth may be literally riddled with these tunnels.

One can recognize a lemming burrow by the freshly turned soil in front of the mouth and by the droppings near it. Most of the burrows which I have opened have contained but a single individual, which would always be hidden in the nest at the end of the tunnel, whence it could watch all my movements. It would not stir while I was opening the entrance corridor or the side-tunnels, but as soon as I touched the nest it would jump like lightning on to my hand. The first few times, when I was not aware of their hasty temper, I was severely bitten. Once it is out of the nest it is almost impossible to get hold of it, for it slips with incredible speed from one tunnel to another, and then disappears completely.

The lemming leaves its burrow principally at night. As far as possible it avoids marshy or even damp ground. One can see traces of its nocturnal wanderings from the tops of the highest mountains right down to the seashore. It even goes on to the nunataks—the mountain summits which emerge from the Inland Ice. In fact it likes all types of country, as long as they are dry and have plenty of plant life.

In winter the lemming manages to get across the snow to reach its feeding-places, as long as the covering is still thin, but its tracks show that it does so only with some difficulty. When the snow is soft lemmings can make progress only by a series of jumps, and once it hardens or becomes more than about eight inches thick they start to disappear underground.

As lemmings do not hibernate or accumulate reserves of food during the summer, they have to search for nourishment throughout the winter. When the immediate neighbourhood of the burrow is exhausted they extend their tunnels, for hundreds of yards, to more distant areas with plant growth. This may mean that they have to cross deep river-beds; in such cases they do not dig along at ground level, but drive through the thickness of the snow. Lemmings thus do a considerable amount of channelling during the course of a winter, but of course they keep warm in their galleries, and are sheltered from the storms and severe weather which the larger animals have to contend with throughout the dark season.

At this time of year it is absolutely essential to the lemmings that the temperature should remain constant at below freezing-point. A sudden strong thaw in the middle of winter would be fatal to the whole lemming population, for the animals would be soaked within their burrows and die of cold. This does happen sometimes at the southern limit of their distribution, around Scoresby Sound and a little to the south, either late in autumn or in the middle of winter. As a result lemmings are completely absent from the area during the succeeding summers.

Page 111. "*I then started to imitate the call of the cock. Consumed with jealousy, he ran twice round the hen . . .*" (p. 151).
          A male ptarmigan.
Page 112. *A female ptarmigan changing to winter plumage.*
          Ptarmigan chicks one day old.

Our knowledge of the habits of the lemming under the winter snow is by no means complete. We do not know, for instance, the function of the nests they build in winter down on the earth. One finds the remains of these nests during the summer; they are usually situated in small depressions in the ground and resemble those which are made in the summer, except that they are much larger. Little piles of excrement around them show that they must have been occupied for a long time. I suppose that if the lemming is for some reason forced to abandon its tunnels it makes a new nest on the surface of the soil itself; it cannot, of course, dig into the frozen soil, and so it makes use of a small natural hole.

At the approach of spring, towards the end of April and well in advance of the thaw, the snow is pierced by small holes through which the lemmings emerge into the daylight. This is the time of courtship, and using its sense of smell the little rodent leaves in search of a mate. If two males meet they fight savagely and no quarter is given, and as though to show his superiority, the winner eats at least half of his rival. I have often found lemmings killed in this way; they were all literally scalped, and they lacked the entrails and part of the breast.

Lemmings are most intolerant beasts, and they can be more savage than the most bloodthirsty carnivore. When several of them are kept captive in the same cage scarcely a day passes without the weakest ones being killed and partly eaten. This fratricidal struggle goes on until finally only the strongest remains.

At the beginning of spring lemmings start to breed under the snow. Evidence from captive animals shows that they may have up to five litters in a year. In some years they become so numerous that one is almost stepping on them. On these occasions, which are known as good lemming years, they undertake mass migrations.

Page 113. *An Arctic tern sitting on its eggs, showing clearly the circle of pebbles which surrounds them.*
The terns are indefatigable travellers.
Page 114. *A female Arctic tern, which nests right on the ground.*

F

I was able to observe this curious phenomenon in Scoresby Sound during the winter of 1927–28, when it happened in the middle of winter and at the beginning of spring. Suddenly, in the middle of January, the lemmings moved across the frozen ice of Scoresby Sound. Day by day their numbers increased, and soon their tracks were to be found all over the surface of the fjord. Travelling by sledge in the area, it was extremely difficult to control the dogs and keep them from chasing lemmings, which were gambolling in front of them like little white goblins. Those which were crossing near the mouth of the fjord were stopped in the middle by open water. Instead of following round the edge of the ice to get to the other side of the fjord, they tried to jump from the firm ice on to pieces of drift-ice. Many fell into the water and swam valiantly, but most of them perished. I believe that not a single one succeeded in crossing the mouth of the fjord, for sooner or later they would have had to negotiate a stretch of sea six miles wide before they could reach the other side. Those which did not fall into the water were hunted by ravens, snowy owls, and foxes.

This migration did not seem noticeably to have affected the strength of the lemming population in the area. In the succeeding summer they seemed as numerous as ever, but in the following spring there was a change, presumably produced in the course of the winter; only a few tunnels were found in the snow, and not a single winter nest. In this year there was not a single lemming to be seen. Their total disappearance remains a mystery.

The lemming has numerous enemies and is, in fact, the most persecuted of all polar animals. The fox and the ermine feed on it almost exclusively, and the polar bear and wolf hunt it occasionally. The snowy owl and the long-tailed skua are very fond of eating it, and so are ravens, falcons, and glaucous gulls. In years when lemmings are scarce their enemies also suffer. The fox has to kill its cubs, and is lucky if it can raise even one or two of them. The ermine either does not breed or else she abandons her young. The snowy owl feeds only the strongest of her chicks, or she may, like the ermine, not breed at all. On their arrival in Greenland at the beginning of June the skuas are soon aware of the absence of lemmings, and they leave again. When, however, the lemmings are abundant all these predators make up for the bad times. The vixen may have up to twelve cubs and raise them all. The ermine has six, and the snowy owl and the long-tailed skua both breed success-fully. By the autumn there are young animals everywhere, and that is when one uses the term 'a good lemming year.' Among those who also profit are the hunters, for in such years the trapping of foxes pays handsomely.

The ermine of Greenland is not very different from that of Scandi-navia. Its winter coat is a little longer and more compact, while in summer its fur is a slightly paler shade of chestnut. In habits it is similar to its European cousin, and it is not specially adapted for Arctic life. In winter it has to seek protection from the cold in holes in the snow or under stones. Ermines captured in traps during the winter usually die of cold in the course of the night. They are never abundant, but they are widely distributed. In winter they hunt the lemmings in their tunnels, and catch them easily, but are unable to slip through the very narrow burrows. In the height of summer they often hunt lemmings by silently approaching the mouth of a burrow and pushing in the front part of the body, hoping, no doubt, that the lemming may, by chance, be near the entrance. Actually, this often happens, for the lemming when taken by surprise, has a marked tendency to defend itself instead of running away. When it is outside its burrow the lem-ming seems to feel quite safe when it has only its head hidden under a stone or in a small hole. When the lemming is out feeding, the ermine will hunt right through the night, and during summer it will also look for birds' nests, from which it takes eggs and chicks, and, being capable of great speed, it even catches young birds after they have left the nest, and also the adults of small species. The ermine also eats carrion, and in winter it will remove the baits from fox traps, and is often caught in them—much to the annoyance of the trappers.

The Walrus

OF ALL the marine mammals of the Arctic Ocean the walrus is the nearest to the true terrestrial animals, for, although well adapted for life in the water, it cannot completely dispense with the dry land. It differs from the seals in that it can turn the hind-limbs forward, and this allows it to raise itself up and gives it greater freedom of movement on land; the true seals, on the other hand, are better swimmers.

In size the walrus varies from one region of the Arctic to another. Those in Canada may be fifteen feet long, while those in North-east Greenland have not, as far as I know, been known to exceed a length of twelve feet from the muzzle to the tip of the tail. An average beast will measure about nine feet. The front flippers are twenty-five inches long and the back ones about twenty inches. The female is rarely longer than nine feet.

The walrus is covered by a thick layer of fat and an extraordinarily tough leathery skin. The covering of hairs on the skin is sparse; in the adults these are light brown, while in the young they are almost dark green. The head is small in relation to the heavy, clumsy body, but it does form the most characteristic feature of the animal. The upper lip is thick and fleshy, and has a stiff moustache, the bristles of which are directed downward and are longer at the corners of the mouth. The canine teeth of the upper jaw are elongated to form tusks which extend in front of the lower jaw, and may reach a length of twenty-seven inches in the male. Males can be distinguished at a distance from females by the form of the tusks. In both sexes they are slightly curved in towards the body, but in the male they are thicker at the base and are almost parallel to each other along the whole of their length, whereas in the female they are often twice as far apart at the tips as they are at the bases, and their length does not normally exceed twelve to fourteen inches. All the same, the shape and position of these defensive weapons may vary in both males and females. Sometimes the tips converge, and may even touch each other, or one tusk may be longer than the other. Quite often they are damaged, with the tip broken, or one may be completely lacking. Sometimes very old walruses have lost both tusks.

The voice of the walrus is certainly the loudest to be heard in the wastes of the Arctic. In calm weather it can be heard at a distance of several miles. It is a strong, abrupt bellow or sometimes a bark. On land the walrus expresses his wellbeing by a series of groans and grunts and sighs of satisfaction.

In summer walruses may be seen all along the north-east coast, but nowhere are they abundant, and they do not appear to have any permanent homes, such as are known on the west coast. Sometimes one finds them gathered together in areas which they will suddenly abandon and not revisit. In fact, it is almost impossible to give an area where one can be certain of finding them during the summer.

In winter and spring they frequent stretches of open water, the distribution of which varies from year to year. All the same, there are certain places where they are more common—for example, the mouth of Scoresby Sound, the waters round Sabine Island and Borlase Warren, and those near Shannon and Koldewey Islands. In these places one can be certain of finding walruses every winter. They disperse at the beginning of spring, when the open water extends up to the shore, but they always remain near the coast. This is doubtless because they search for their food on the sea-bottom and avoid great depths. At any rate, it is rare to find a walrus more than ten sea miles from land.

Their favourite places are the shores of Sabine Island, the mouth of Young Inlet, and Dove Bay, where I once saw forty-eight of them, as I will describe later in the chapter, and where some Norwegian hunters killed thirty-seven in the course of a single spring. They also used to be abundant in Scoresby Sound, until the Greenlanders started to hunt them.

Walruses live in families, consisting of a male, two or three females, and their young. They remain together in a group, both in the water and on the ice. The male is a very conscientious leader and defender of the family. He will not tolerate any strange intruder, and always keeps an eye out for solitary males, who never miss a chance to sow discord.

The young are born out on the ice in April, and while they are still small the whole family remains there. From time to time one of the adults takes a swim, diving right down to the bottom, but without going far away. The young are never left completely alone.

While the male is always on the watch for possible enemies the females busy themselves with their offspring. At times when a youngster is not sleeping or suckling the mother allows it to crawl over her, or she plays with it, holding it between her front flippers and lifting it into the air, or she may give it a bath. From a distance one can hear the yelling of the babies, mingled with the contented grunts of their elders. Once the young have passed the infant stage the parents push them into the water, where they swim round the floe, bawling, until their mother takes pity on them and lifts them back on to the ice. If, for any reason, the family has to leave the ice-floe the females take their young between their front flippers and carry them thus, while swimming on their backs. They do the same when a young one has been shot, and a female carrying a dead young one in this way may attack the hunter.

By the summer the young are already sufficiently grown to follow their parents on trips along the coast and into the fjords, but they are by no means able to fend for themselves. They are fed by the mother for a year and a half, and take even longer than the polar bear to become independent, and, in fact, the adults breed only every third year. But walruses do-not live only in family parties; sometimes one may come across big groups composed entirely of males.

In the summer of 1925, during the Scoresby Sound Expedition, one of my companions and I had the unpleasant experience of finding ourselves suddenly surrounded by a family of walruses. We were crossing Rosenvinge Bay in a rowing-boat when a walrus surfaced just in front of us. He came up only for a moment, and then quietly disappeared. In the calm water we could see him below us, swimming on his back, so that the tusks were clearly visible. We were scarcely twenty yards from the nearest ice-floe. To seek refuge there was our only means of escaping from this monster, but just as the oars touched the water the boat was jolted so violently that we both fell off our seats, and immediately afterwards another blow nearly threw us overboard. The walrus surfaced and came right alongside the boat. We had to ship the oars to avoid touching him, and thus making him even more annoyed. There was nothing else we could do, because our guns would have been useless against such an adversary. We could easily have touched the enormous beast, which was longer than our own boat. His back was above the surface, and his head was raised so high that he could look over the side of the boat. He was an old male with one broken tusk. For two minutes he watched us, and then, curiosity satisfied, he dived, but in so doing gave the stern such a blow with his hind-flippers that water splashed into the boat. If the blow had come on the side the boat would certainly have been stove in.

Temporarily, at least, we were out of danger, but as we rowed as fast as we could towards the ice-floe walruses appeared all around us. We were in the territory of a family consisting of four adults and three young. Our previous visitor had been the leader, whom we now recognized by his broken tusk.

As though at a given signal, the whole family assembled in a group and followed us. We reached the floe and hauled the boat ashore.

The walruses came right up to the edge of our sanctuary, the male even putting his flippers over the edge and pulling himself partly out of the water. One of the females dived under the floe, while the other two kept close to the male and grunted. We then pulled the boat for about two hundred yards across the ice-floe, and, having made certain that the walruses had not followed us under the ice, we covered the last hundred yards which separated us from the shore, rowing as fast as we could. Before we had drawn the boat on land, however, we saw the whole family again, in the water beneath us, their dark bodies clearly distinguishable against the light sand; a little later they surfaced, snorting and groaning and spraying us with water. The old male hauled himself ashore, and, for no apparent reason, gave out a roar which echoed in the mountains. We finished the rest of our journey dragging the boat along the water's edge.

On the following day when we were returning to the headquarters of the expedition, at Amdrups Harbour, and passing the same place, we saw the walruses on an ice-floe in the distance. The male had already seen us, for he had lifted himself up on to his flippers, and, high above the others, was watching attentively. We were rowing along the water's edge so as to be ready to jump ashore if it became necessary— and it was. As soon as he saw us approaching he slipped silently into the water, and we soon saw him passing by like a shadow over the pale sand. By then we had already reached the shore and had pulled the boat to a safe place. As on the previous day, he came ashore and barked with indignation, but, being powerless on dry land, he soon returned to his real element. It was, however, an hour before we could proceed on our way, for the watchful beast remained near by, and

Page 123. *Nothing can separate the red-throated diver from its chicks.*
    When it sees an intruder the red-throated diver stretches its head out over the edge of the nest.
Page 124. *The red-throated diver comes up close to the nest.*
    Before sitting down to brood it turns the eggs over.
    It incubates with head erect and lifts its sharp, menacing beak against anyone who approaches the nest.

every time we tried to launch the boat he surfaced from the depths. Finally he left us and returned to his ice-floe.

On another occasion I was spending a week with one of my companions while the expedition moved farther to the north. We decided to go to the hunting depot in Dove Bay, which is the northernmost one in North-east Greenland. The three hunters who had spent the winter there were told of our coming by the ship's radio, and were ahead of us. We met them half-way along the route, on the south coast of Germania Land.

After the usual greetings they told us that in travelling along the coast, about an hour's journey from where we were, they had suddenly been attacked by walruses, and the boat had almost capsized. Owing to the lightness of their craft, they had not dared to shoot and had reached the shore only with difficulty. About one and a quarter miles farther along the shore they had found a big herd of about fifty walruses sleeping on dry land. They had been able to walk up close without any of them showing signs of returning to the water.

We all agreed to go immediately to have a look at these walruses. The sight of this large group of marine mammals stretched out on the ground would be most impressive, and so, guided by the hunters, we sailed along the shore in our motor-boat. Several times we passed walruses asleep on the ice. We tried to approach them, but they always dived before we had reached their ice-floe, and each time they swam towards us, took a turn round the boat, and then disappeared. Soon the hunters told us that we were not far from the place where the walruses were sleeping. They are so like the big boulders scattered on the beach, that it was not until a pair of tusks flashed in the sunlight that we realized that what we had taken for a mass of rocks was, in fact, walruses. Sailing round in a wide circle, we came to land about 500

Page 125. *Eider-ducks in the shallow waters around the island.*
The little long-tailed duck on its nest. Note the down which completely surrounds the bird.
Page 126. *A female eider on her nest.*
Eider-duck nests showing the rim of down.

yards from the animals. We approached them cautiously, keeping ourselves hidden behind boulders. At 200 yards distance they still had not
given any signs of unrest. We were soon close enough to see them all,
and to count 48 animals stretched out in little groups close to one
another. Most of them were lying on their sides or backs, flippers in
the air and fast asleep. They were all adult males. At ten yards distance
we stopped to watch them sleeping.

It was certainly an incredible sight. The walrus can scarcely be described as a beautiful animal, even though its underwater movements have
a certain elegance. Those we now saw stretched before us on the sand,
apparently lifeless, had no resemblance to these animals. They looked
more like enormous masses of dough. The small head was almost
obscured by the large fold of skin covering the neck. When one of
these shapeless objects had to move it would slowly raise its body with
a series of groans, grunts, and sighs, as though the whole process was
a painful effort. We advanced again without their taking any notice.
In front of me lay a male who appeared to be the largest in the group.
I went right up so as to touch him, and eventually he raised his head,
turned over on to his belly, and lifted himself up with some difficulty
on to his flippers. He remained in this position for a moment, looked
at me with tiny eyes, so congested as to appear completely red, and
then, turning his head to one side, he rolled over into his original
position with a big, contented sigh.

Somebody threw a stone the size of a nut at one of the slumberers,
and it had a completely unexpected effect. The walrus quickly raised
his head and planted his tusks into the back of his neighbour, who in
his turn did the same to the next one. Soon the whole group was in
confusion. They rolled around, puffing and grunting, with their white
tusks glistening in the sun like weapons of steel. We retreated in the
face of the enormous forces which we had so unwittingly released.

Suddenly, as though at a given signal, they all started to move
towards the sea. For one moment there was a real *mêlée*, for the animals
in front apparently refused to enter the water, and those who followed
tried to climb over their bodies. Then the whole lot literally rolled

into the sea. But far from disappearing they snorted and turned back towards the shore, forming a long line in the shallow water. Some of them emerged and came up the beach in a menacing way. They were obviously waiting for us to go, before returning to their slumbers, and so we left them in peace. We had scarcely turned our backs before they romped up the beach, and even before we had reached the boat all forty-eight of them were stretched out on the sand fast asleep.

Walruses seem to have a certain dislike of motor-boats. I have never heard of their attacking one as they attack a rowing-boat. Perhaps the noise of the screw in the water keeps them away. I have, however, seen a family of walruses going out to a ship which had dropped anchor. Led by the male, the females and the young ones swam under the ship and then twice round it. The adults lifted themselves out of the water one by one, and finally they all disappeared.

The best way to rid oneself of an inquisitive walrus is to shoot it. But if one is not in a large, solid boat it must be killed at the first shot, otherwise this becomes a sure method of suicide, for a wounded walrus is the most dangerous animal in the Arctic. Instead of escaping, it attacks furiously. Worst of all is when the wounded animal belongs to a family or to a group, because then all its companions come to its help. Only a really strong boat can withstand their attack. Arctic hunters still speak of the time when a crew of eight men was lost in a fight against a group of walruses.

The most vulnerable parts of a walrus are the neck and the temple. A shot in the body, even from close range, is seldom immediately fatal, nor is one aimed at the front of the head, as the bullet glances off the thick bony skull.

A shot walrus sinks immediately, then in the course of twenty-four hours it fills with gas and comes up again to the surface, but in the meantime the body will have drifted away in the currents. The Greenlanders of Scoresby Sound hunt walruses from kayaks, but only the most skilled of them will risk this method. An inexperienced man will sooner carry his kayak overland than risk waters where he may meet a walrus. Experienced hunters either avoid being attacked by a walrus or else kill it before it has a chance to attack. Walrus-hunting by the ancient Eskimos was far more dangerous and difficult, for they had no knowledge of firearms and had only harpoons. Judging from the piles of walrus bones found round the ruins of their encampments in Northeast Greenland, these Eskimos must have hunted them on a big scale, but probably many of the men lost their lives.

From my own observations I can say nothing about the time of mating in walruses or about the period of gestation. During the Danmark Expedition, Frits Johansen saw what he believed to be a mating. Here is his own report, taken from the Danish publication *Meddelelser om Grønland*:

> On August 25, 1907, I saw two walruses in Storm Bay. They were swimming so close to the shore that their bodies appeared above the surface; then they glided out side by side under the thin new ice, and finally came up in a little bay. They snorted and came close to one another, until they lay on their sides, belly to belly, and then sank down in the water. Shortly afterwards they came in sight again in the same position, turned somersaults, and twisted and turned in such a way that it was impossible to distinguish one body from the other. Each time they turned round their heads came close together, until finally each lifted all four flippers vertically into the air. Then they disappeared into the water and came up again in the same way. They stopped after half an hour, but only to swim away to another patch of open water, where the process was repeated.

In Scoresby Sound, on August 29, 1928, I found a dead female walrus which contained a fœtus four and a quarter inches long. From this one must conclude that the mating season extends over a relatively long period.

Natural-history books and the reports of explorers often express the view that the walrus feeds entirely on bivalve molluscs and seaweed, and that it uses its impressive tusks only to dig up vegetation from the sea-bottom, in its search for food. This is not entirely wrong. The walrus does feed principally on bivalves, and is able to reject the indigestible shells; it is also very probable that it uses the tusks to wrench the molluscs from among the algal vegetation on the sea-bottom. It is not, however, vegetarian, and when one finds odd pieces of vegetable matter in the stomach they have been taken in only accidentally, just as one also finds stones up to the size of a fist. The walrus does not, however, feed entirely on molluscs. It also kills seals, whose thick blubber it relishes as a delicacy. There have hitherto been a number of erroneous ideas on this subject. The remains of seals found in the stomachs of walruses have been thought to come from seals which the walrus has found dead. The Danmark Expedition killed a walrus which contained seal remains, and Frits Johansen, who describes the incident, says that they were the remains of a polar bear's prey found by the walrus on the ice, and he adds that there is naturally no evidence that the walrus killed the seal. Farther on in this report, however, which contains much of value on the walrus in North-east Greenland, he describes an observation made in Amdrup Land, which clearly shows that a walrus can kill a seal:

On the ice, very close to a stretch of open water, we saw a walrus and a ringed seal not far from each other. The walrus was near a hole in the ice, which was probably the one from which the seal had emerged. When the men approached both animals made off towards the open water, but the walrus was faster, and he caught up with the seal and struck his tusks into its back. Both animals were later killed.

From my own observations I am convinced that the walrus often eats seals, particularly young ringed seals. I have twice seen a walrus chase and kill them. Evidently they prefer to hunt in the water; they swim on their backs and glide beneath the seal at the moment when the latter is lifting its head out of the water to breathe. Then they seize the prey between their front flippers and strike with the tusks. Probably the seal is killed immediately by this powerful attack. This was shown by my examination of one of the victims: the backbone was broken and the breast ripped open. The walrus always makes for the nearest ice-floe, holding the prey between its forelimbs. It pushes the carcass ashore, and then hauls itself out. Then it uses the tusks to open the whole length of the belly, and eats large pieces of the blubber with the attached skin. It does the dismemberment entirely with the tusks, as the blunt molars are not adapted for such a task. The greater part of the carcass is left untouched, and in examinations of the stomach contents of walruses the only seal remains I have found have been large pieces of blubber and skin and, on one occasion, a complete flipper.

The walrus is not able to live under the permanent winter ice, and this is why it is not found in the fjord at this time of year; it is unable to keep open a breathing-hole in the ice as the seals do. However, in places where the ice is thin it can open up a little bay in the following way: it lies close under the surface of the ice, then arches its back, and straightens out again in such a way that the top of the skull strikes the ice with a sudden blow. It does this several times until the ice is shattered, and if it is going to stay in the same place for some time it enlarges the hole with its teeth. Then each time it comes to the spot to breathe—the normal duration of a dive is about ten minutes—it again breaks the thin skin of ice which has re-formed. In the middle of winter these walrus holes can be found right along the coast, especially in places where a strong current prevents the formation of thick ice. The holes may be up to twelve feet in diameter, and often form the permanent home of a family or of a little group.

At the beginning of winter it sometimes happens that a walrus becomes imprisoned in a bay or fjord. It may have stayed too long in a patch of open water, and the ice may have formed so quickly that it cannot break it. If then its food-supply on the sea-bottom becomes exhausted the walrus will die of starvation, unless it can reach another area. When such areas are far distant the animal has to make a painful journey over the ice. One walrus which had to travel thirty miles in this way became so emaciated that it had absolutely no fat under the skin, and the latter was worn through in several places on the belly. This starving animal allowed itself to be killed, without offering any resistance, by an Eskimo who had followed its very obvious tracks in the snow.

The Seals

THERE ARE four species of seals living in the Greenland area, in addition to the walrus. Two of these, the bladdernose seal (*Cystophora cristata*) and the Greenland seal (*Phoca groenlandica*), are remarkably fine swimmers, which go far out into the Arctic Ocean, suckle their young on drifting ice-floes, and only occasionally approach the coasts of Greenland. They are unable to live under the fast ice, and so they rarely enter the fjords and bays, which are completely ice-bound in winter.

On the other hand, the ringed seal (*Phoca foetida*) and the bearded seal (*Erignathus barbatus*) live the whole time close to the coast and in the bays and fjords. Throughout the winter they are able to stay beneath the ice, owing to their astonishing ability to keep open holes for breathing. They are hunted regularly by the Eskimos, for whom they form the staple diet.

The bearded seal is the largest of the four seals, and it reaches a length of more than nine feet. It owes its Scandinavian name of 'Remmesael' (literally 'thong seal') to the strong thongs which the Greenlanders cut from its skin for their hunting equipment. Elsewhere they are known as bearded seals, from their thick moustaches. They occur along almost the whole of the Greenland coast, particularly on the east coast and on the northern part of the west coast. By preference they stay in fairly shallow water, where they can hunt crustaceans on the bottom. This is why there was a considerable stir in 1937–38, when the Russians, during their drift on the ice from the North Pole, reported a bearded seal in a hole in the ice in latitude 88° N. Previously Fridtjof Nansen's expedition had killed one in 85° N.

The bearded seal is much hunted wherever it is found, and in Greenland the majority of seals killed by Europeans belong to this species. One can approach quite close to them in spring and the beginning of summer, when they are out on the ice undergoing their annual moult. In such circumstances I have been able to creep up to within ten paces of them, and a boat can also approach as close as this before they make up their minds to dive. They will enter the water only when forced to and when their pelts are dry. The majority moult in spring and at the beginning of summer, but one can still see old seals moulting in the second half of summer. This means that it is perfectly possible to hunt bearded seals throughout spring and summer, and, of course, their natural enemy, the polar bear, also takes his share.

When it is no longer worried by the moult the bearded seal changes its behaviour, and ceases to be idle and somnolent. It becomes as watchful and shy as the other Arctic seals, spending most of its time in the water, preferably at the mouth of a river, where it catches the small fish which form a considerable part of its diet. On the coast of Siberia, where large rivers flow into the Arctic Ocean, the bearded seals travel far up their course in pursuit of fish, but in Greenland they remain in the estuaries and in the neighbouring shallow waters. When swimming on the surface they are easily recognizable, because the neck and a narrow strip of the back are visible above the water. In places where they are much hunted one can get within gun range only with some difficulty,

Page 135. *The nest of a pink-footed goose. The eggs are laid on a bedding of down and dry grass.*
   A couple of pink-footed geese.
Page 136. *The nest of a barnacle goose on a ledge.*
   A barnacle goose and its nest perched on an inaccessible cliff.

in spite of the fact that they are not particularly good swimmers. Their hearing, on the other hand, is excellent, and they are not so shortsighted as the other seals, nor so inquisitive as the ringed seals. They are usually shot when they put their heads out of water to breathe, but even then there is no hope of getting hold of them if they are seen to sink immediately, and they sink very fast in the fresh waters off the river-mouths.

Only the Eskimos manage to hunt them successfully in the water, using a combination of gun and harpoon. They are well aware, however, that old bearded seals may be dangerous—a point which I myself was able to confirm during a kayak trip with the Eskimos of Scoresby Sound.

We were forcing a way in our delicate kayaks through the drift-ice off the low sandy coast and had entered a patch of open water at the mouth of a large river, when one of the Greenlanders, who was out in front, saw a bearded seal. He harpooned it on the spot. While waiting for it to resurface he had his gun ready so as to kill it with a shot. Suddenly, in the clear water, he saw the seal coming up below his kayak, evidently intending to tear the thin skin covering of the craft with its sharp claws. With a few quick strokes of the paddle he moved off, but when he stopped the seal was again beneath him. Being unable to kill the angry seal while it was still submerged, he paddled along a large floe, and got his kayak on to a piece of ice which jutted out under the water. There he waited for a moment, hoping that the seal—whose position he knew from the floating bladder attached to the harpoon line—would quieten down as it became tired. When he ventured out into the open water again the animal was beneath him, and once more he had to zigzag to avoid its furious attacks. Finally, the seal had to surface in order to breathe. In a split second the Greenlander changed paddle for gun, took aim, and shot it. This seal was an old male, with a pelt showing many wound marks as evidence of its bellicose nature.

Later on in the autumn I took part in an exciting and unusual hunt for bearded and ringed seals off the foot of a glacier, in a bay on the

Page 137. *The large yellow flowers of the Arctic poppy.*
Page 138. *A calm summer day in a fjord in North-east Greenland.*

G

Liverpool coast—a spot with a bad reputation which faces directly on to the Arctic Ocean. The bay was covered with a mirror of ice, and there was not a breath of wind. There were three of us, the two Eskimos—Emil and Manasse—and myself. We had left our sledge and dogs on the shore, and had donned our kamiks—Eskimo boots of bear-skin made with the fur outside—which allowed us to walk absolutely silently over the thin, polished ice.

We went forward for a certain distance, and then stopped for a moment to listen. The seals had made their holes in the ice. Holding our breath, we could hear them blowing farther out in the bay. They were ringed seals, but the Greenlanders thought that there might also be some bearded seals among them.

We moved towards the glacier, where most of them seemed to be. Their breathing became more and more audible. Suddenly the Greenlanders stopped again to listen. They had heard two bearded seals, but from different directions. The breathing of the bearded seal is a little stronger and longer than that of the ringed seal, although I could not tell the difference. The Greenlanders split up, each going to his own seal. I followed Emil. While actually breathing a seal does not hear what is going on around it, so we were able to walk forward for a few minutes, but each time we heard it stop breathing we stood absolutely still.

Each seal has several breathing-holes usually quite near to one another, although they may be far apart, even up to half a mile away. The seals visit these holes at regular intervals, and so one must be prepared to wait for a long time, particularly if the animal has been disturbed near the last hole it has visited.

We were lucky. At the end of about ten minutes the seal had returned. I was now able to appreciate the difference between the breathing of the bearded seal and that of the ringed seals which we could hear all around. Whilst I remained quite still, Emil circled round so that the low, dull sun was facing him—in this way he would not be preceded by his own shadow—and then walked up quickly towards the breathing-hole. He had not quite reached it when the seal stopped blowing. The final part of its breathing was quite normal, so it had not yet become suspicious. This time almost twenty minutes elapsed before it returned—twenty mintues during which we had to remain absolutely still. During this time the seal must have visited its other holes. Emil allowed it to breathe a few times before going right up to the hole. Then he took his harpoon in both hands and thrust it sharply into the hole, which was only a few inches across. He held the seal by the line attached to the harpoon while he enlarged the hole with his knife. I rejoined him and took the line, while he gave the seal a final blow. After we had made the hole large enough we hauled the dead animal out on to the ice.

At this moment we saw Manasse in the distance. Leaving our seal there, we continued the hunt until nightfall, by which time Emil had also killed three ringed seals. For one of these he used a kind of trick to give confidence to a seal which apparently did not wish to return to the hole. I suppose he did this for my sake, for he knew that I wanted to learn everything about their habits and the methods of hunting. When he considered that he had waited long enough he carefully went up to the hole, knelt down, and used his hunting-knife to peck gently at the ice, while imitating the croaking of a raven. This bird often catches crustaceans and small fish in the breathing-holes of seals, and the idea is that the seal, hearing this activity, is reassured that none of its enemies are in the immediate neighbourhood. Naturally I cannot say whether the seal returned for this reason, or whether it would have come back without it, but at any rate it did return and was harpooned.

If only the days had not been so short we could have gone for much longer. When we got back to the shore Manasse was already there, with three more ringed seals.

According to the Greenlanders, hunting on 'the smooth ice' is the easiest form of seal-hunting, and if conditions are right it cannot fail to give good results. Generally, however, it can be done only over a period of a few days. Once the ice is covered with snow, or when ice crystals have formed, it is too late. This is what happened on this occasion. The following night it snowed, and the 'smooth-ice' hunting was finished for that year.

The Ptarmigan

Comparison between the mammals and the birds of the high Arctic reveals the scarcity of the latter. Being able to leave the Arctic as soon as the climate becomes too unfavourable, many birds have little need to adapt themselves to it. In this chapter I will not discuss these migratory birds, which live there only during the summer, but rather the true polar birds, such as the ptarmigans, snowy owls, and ravens.

Of the three the ptarmigan is the most hardy. It never leaves the most northerly regions, and can spend the winter at latitude 75° N., where the polar night lasts for three months. It is, in fact, the only bird which lives permanently in North-east Greenland, for the snowy owl and the raven spend the winter down on the Arctic Circle, or perhaps even a little bit farther south.

The ptarmigan is the most northerly representative of the gallinaceous birds—a group which includes the jungle fowl and pheasants—and there is no other land bird which ventures so far north. Thanks to a thick coat of feathers, which covers it right down to the claws, it can withstand the icy climate, and is also able to survive on the very poor vegetation which it finds in winter. Among the birds of the high Arctic, it occupies a position exactly comparable with that of the hare, among the mammals. Both have a winter coat as white as snow, and both live in the same areas and feed on the same plants.

During the polar night ptarmigan live in groups, and by preference at altitudes where there are snow-free areas. Even before the return of the sun great flights of ptarmigan move northward, not following the coast like the migratory birds, but going along the edge of the Inland Ice. Their journey finished, they disperse in groups of five to ten, and settle on the mountain slopes which are free from snow. About a month after the return of the sun ptarmigan are found everywhere— except in the lower regions which are still covered deep in snow—and settle both in the interior near the Inland Ice and on the coast. They feed, often in the mornings, on the shoots of willows and other plants, and are so preoccupied that one can approach to within a few feet of them before they scatter, rather like domestic fowls, to avoid being trampled on. Their white plumage makes them look like the few remaining patches of snow, and often you do not see them until they dart out suddenly from under your feet. At night they shelter under large stones, in rock crevices, or in small holes made by themselves in the snow. Their nocturnal shelters can be recognized by the small deposits of droppings which carpet the floor.

The first calls of the cock ptarmigan are heard in the middle of April. At the end of the month the groups divide into pairs, each taking up its own territory, but another month goes by before egg-laying begins. The hen bird has now acquired her summer plumage, which blends as well with the colour of the earth as does her winter plumage with the snow.

All summer, which lasts for half the year, she moults continuously, her plumage always adapting itself to its natural background, while the male does not lose his winter dress until July. During the time the cocks are mounting guard over the brooding hen they remain conspicuously white, and as a result are captured in their thousands by birds of prey. So numerous are the males, however, that the females are compensated for such losses right up to the end of the lay. One wonders what would happen if the retarded moult of the cocks did not help to draw danger away from the nests. Seeing the dazzling white males sitting in full view during the incubation period, one has the impression that they voluntarily attract attention to themselves.

The hen bird has no trouble in placing her nest, usually in a dry spot among the crowberry or dwarf willow, or, failing that, among the stones. She makes a small depression, if there is not already one there, and lays six to twelve eggs, whose spotted shells cannot be distinguished from their surroundings. Indeed, one very rarely finds them.

She is very vigilant. To avoid betraying its position a hen never openly leaves or returns to her nest, and is aided in these stealthy manœuvres by her concealing plumage. If frightened she runs in a wide semicircle away from the nest to put the intruder off the trail, and only then takes flight. The male always stays a short distance away, taking up a fixed position, often on top of a big stone, whence he can view the surrounding area and warn the hen of an approaching enemy. When she leaves the nest for exercise or food, usually in the afternoon, the cock does not follow her until she is some distance from the nest.

Towards the middle of the incubation period the cock disappears. He flies up into the mountains to change his winter plumage—whose original whiteness has become a little soiled—for a summer one. This differs from that of the hen in being finer and softer, and in that his belly and wings remain white.

The incubation period lasts for twenty-one days. As soon as the newly hatched chicks are dry they are able to run about, and the mother immediately takes them away from the nest and tends them constantly during the first few days. Many times during the day, and every night, she calls them back to brood them under her wings. If an enemy approaches, the chicks, warned by the anxious clucking of their mother, scatter surreptitiously to shelter among the stones, exactly like the very young Arctic hares. The hen then takes flight, attracting the attention of the enemy and drawing him away from her young, and returns only when the danger has passed.

After the first few days the chicks become astonishingly active, and from the eighth day they start to use their wings. When danger threatens they disperse in all directions. The hens look after their young until they are able to fly properly. By the end of autumn, after numerous moults, the chicks have white flight feathers, white feathers on the feet, and closely resemble their parents.

All the ptarmigan, young and adult, lose their dark summer plumage in the course of September and assume the white feathers of winter.

In the spring of 1932 I was visiting the station of the Nanok Hunting Company at Sandodden, on Wollaston Foreland. In my daily trips towards the eastern part of this area I saw on several occasions a white ptarmigan, always sitting on the same stone. At my approach he would turn his head and look at me, but never left his observation post. Next time I was there it occurred to me that there must be a pair of them, and that the female was certainly somewhere in the neighbourhood. It was still too early for her to have started to lay, but I decided to revisit them when my work allowed me the time.

I was approaching the spot, in the shelter of some boulders, when suddenly the cock saw me and gave out an attenuated call—a sign doubtless understood by the hen. I knew, from many attempts to take close-ups of birds, that I must give them time to get used to my presence, so I sat down on a stone and started to search for the hen. In vain I examined every square inch of the ground with my field-glasses. I then watched the cock, still with my field-glasses, although he was not more than ten yards from me, and soon realized that his indolence was only apparent. Back turned, he none the less kept a wary eye on me. I noticed that the almost imperceptible movements of his head corresponded with any slight gesture I might make, and that he was very much alert. After watching for a moment I realized that I was not the only object of his attention, but that he kept an eye on a spot just in front of me, a little lower down the slope. I looked in this direction and suddenly saw a movement close to a small stone. The hen bird was sitting there, quietly preening.

Having found the exact spot, I approached cautiously step by step. The cock let me go forward some yards, without showing any sign of flight, but called to warn his mate of the approaching danger. She did not stir, except to draw closer to the stone and lie there quietly. It was not until I was some three yards from her that she pulled herself up to her full height, lifted the tips of her wings above her tail, and walked off with a clucking sound. A little farther on she stopped to see whether I was following. As I had not moved, she sat down and returned to her toilet. I then went towards the cock, to see how close I could get to photograph him. Still on his stone, he showed no fear when he saw me approaching, and was apparently quite unconcerned. When there was not more than two yards between us he raised his head in protest, but did not seem to want to fly away, and he let me approach one step nearer. My purpose fulfilled, I withdrew to leave the bird in peace.

Eight days later I was able to see my ptarmigans again. I searched the ground with my field-glasses, and saw them both browsing at the foot of the slope. This time I walked straight towards the hen, who was feeding on willow-leaves at the edge of a stream newly replenished by the melting snow. She was not at all surprised to see me approaching, and when I was not more than two paces away she looked at me over her shoulder, and then went on browsing. Evidently she was quite indifferent to my presence, and I concluded that she had not yet started to lay. When I knelt down to photograph her she let out a call, or rather a miaow, to which the cock replied with a deep and long *grrr*. Some moments later I heard the deep voice of the cock again, but this time from just behind me. When I turned round he came running towards me through the crowberries, tail spread and wings trailing. This was quite another bird from the indifferent gentleman who had previously sat on top of the boulder and appeared so unconcerned at my presence. He came right up to me, and then went over to stand beside the hen. On his arrival, head proudly erect, she crouched down in amorous mood near him. The cock's jealousy was evident. When I

Page 147. *Glaucous Gull chicks in the shelter of a rock.*
　　　　The glaucous gull feeds not only on the young of other birds, but also on dead animals. Here is one on the carcass of a walrus.
Page 148. *In the interior of well-sheltered fjords there is abundant vegetation, composed largely of cotton-grass.*

stood up he tried to position himself between the hen and me. The
nearer I approached, the greater was his annoyance. As his anger
increased, so did the hen increase her pleading, extending her wings,
flattening herself against the ground, and mewing seductively. In the
course of this courtship mating took place. I then started to imitate the
call of the cock. Consumed with jealousy, he ran twice round the
hen, wings drooping, before jumping on to a neighbouring stone. His
every movement betrayed the most violent anger. Several times he
answered the calls of his supposed rival, never taking his eye off him;
he then rejoined the hen. A little later I played the same trick again,
but this time imitated the mewing of the hen. That amorous lady
became as taut as a bowstring, and listened attentively. But, more
intelligent than the cock, she soon understood the source of the call,
and, bursting with rage, came right up to deposit on the tip of my boot
the full expression of her disdain.

Although ptarmigans are never really wild, they are not all as fearless with humans. Two days later I returned to my friends, and saw
the cock at a distance. He was in his usual place and, as before, allowed
me to approach quite near him. The hen was nowhere to be seen, and I
supposed that she had started to lay. I sat down near the cock, hoping
that his behaviour would show me the position of the nest. I watched
him for half an hour, but he was obviously well aware of my intention;
he just sat calmly on his stone, as though sleeping, but nevertheless
keeping a careful look-out. Unable to learn anything from him, I
searched minutely every bit of ground where the hen might conceiv-
ably have her nest. As I did so I kept one eye on the cock in case he
should become restive and warn the hen of my approach—but in vain.
It seemed, moreover, that the cock was trying to hoodwink me, for he

Page 149. *A ringed plover on its nest.*
        Eggs of the ringed plover in their nest of pebbles.
Page 150. *Sanderling chicks, only twenty-four hours old. They have already left
        the nest and are concealing themselves among the leaves of the dwarf
        willow.*
        A sanderling near its nest.

flew off and sat on a stone farther down the slope. At once I thought
that he might join up with the hen there, and that I might then be able
to keep her in sight with my field-glasses until she had shown me the
nest; but nothing happened. Taking flight again, the cock returned to
his former observation post. I gave up at last, and never, in fact,
succeeded in finding the nest, even though on the following day there
were four of us searching the area. I saw the cock again in the first days
of July, shortly before my departure from Sandodden. His presence
there suggested that the hen was not dead, as I had been led to believe,
but that she was incubating somewhere in the neighbourhood.

After my stay at Wollaston Foreland I spent several weeks in
Clavering Island, where I had the good fortune to find several ptarmigans in an unusual domestic setting. Two hens and their chicks had
gathered in the ruins of an Eskimo settlement, not far from the beach,
which had been partly excavated by two ethnographers who had been
camping there since the spring. One day, in the first half of July, these
two discovered that a female ptarmigan had installed her chicks in the
ruins. The birds had been timid at first, but, suffering no harm, had
soon got used to the presence of men. Some time later another hen
and her chicks had arrived from the mountains, and they in turn
had established themselves in the same spot. They also became do-
mesticated in the course of a few days, and were accepted into the
family.

When I arrived the chicks were already past the first stages of growth.
Their wings were large enough to allow them to hop with some
effort on to a two-foot-high wall. One clutch had nine chicks and the
other ten. The dry, soft sand which covered the floor of the ruins and
the coolness they found within during the warm hours of the day
seemed to be the things which particularly attracted them to the place.
While the mothers stayed on the piles of earth thrown up by the
excavations and kept a look-out over the ruins, the chicks took their
sand baths. These ptarmigans were astonishingly tame. One could sit
at the edge of the ruins and watch them close at hand, without their
taking the slightest notice. If some minor crisis arose—if, for instance,

two young cocks were quarrelling—the mothers would stretch their necks the better to see what was going on down in the ruins.

From dawn to dusk the two families browsed in the neighbourhood. At first the chicks kept near their mothers, but as they came to know the place well they undertook their own little foraging expeditions. Twice on these occasions the chicks ventured into the tents and rummaged happily about among the cases and sleeping-bags. Another time a chick took a sand-bath just at the entrance of the tent.

Finally, the chicks were fully fledged, and one evening, quite by chance, I was witness to the departure of the two families. They had gone to their usual feeding-place, but, instead of returning to the ruins, the two hens walked in the opposite direction towards the top of a slope, and suddenly flew off towards a steep cliff. The chicks followed, and I saw the two families line up on the edge of the cliff.

All at once the two mothers took off in a low flight, hugging the cliff face for a hundred yards or so and then regaining the summit. The idea was evidently that the young should make their first aerial expedition, and most of them did very well. Some came down at the foot of the cliff, but quickly took off again and rejoined the others. When all were back on the cliff again the manoeuvre was repeated, and before long I lost sight of them. They never did return, and our ruins seemed quite deserted.

A Paradise for Sea Birds

In THE mouth of Tyrol Fjord, not far from Cape Berghaus, there is a small flat island called Sandö (Sand Island). It is so small that one can walk round it in half an hour. As its name suggests, it consists entirely of sand and gravel, and it is so low-lying that during the autumn storms drift-ice piles up on its coasts, which are thus hidden until the following spring.

Among many similar islands in North-east Greenland I have never seen one which had a comparable population of birds. Every spring thousands of sea birds arrive there, as though to a place of rest after their long migration across the Atlantic. Many of them breed there, and remain throughout the summer.

Sea birds always prefer islands to the mainland, for there they have access to the sea on all sides, and are less exposed to attacks and egg-stealing by the foxes. Sandö provides even more for the birds. It gives them a fine beach of sand, dotted with round white pebbles brought there and deposited by the ice, which is just what aquatic birds like. The centre of the island is covered by a sward formed from innumerable tufts and cushions of moss. In the southern half this mossy carpet borders a small lake of fresh water, and there are several other ponds throughout the island. The sea around is quite shallow. The beach slopes down gently to it, and great depths are reached only at some distance away. This means that thick ice cannot drift close to the shore in summer, and so there is always a wide stretch of open water round the island. The little strait which separates the island from the mainland is so shallow that a large boat cannot pass through at low tide.

The first time I landed there I immediately noticed stones grouped in pairs, without being able to understand how they came to be so arranged. On my second visit I saw eider-ducks crouching between them, and I realized that these were artificial shelters which could have been made only by the Eskimos. As far as I know such bird shelters have never previously been found in areas formerly inhabited by Eskimos. The nearest place they are used is in Iceland. At some former time, therefore, the island must have been inhabited by a family of Eskimos, and, in fact, the ruins of their primitive earth hut are still visible, situated at the highest point on the island, about fifteen feet above sea-level, and covered now with a thick growth of moss and grass. The eiders have taken possession of it as a breeding site, and year after year have made nests in little moss-lined holes between the stones which once formed the roof. One will never know whether the Eskimos lived there for more than one winter. They had, however, established little depots around the hut in which they had, presumably, stored away eggs during the summer, which makes one believe they may have lived there for some time.

During winter the whole island is covered in snow, in spite of the high winds which blow over it. There is no shelter at all, and so it is not surprising that there are no living animals on the island at this time of year.

In spring the snow starts to melt during the warmer hours of the day, and the island receives its first visitors. These are the mysterious brent geese, on their way to nest, we know not where, in the north-east of Greenland. They travel in small parties along the coast. Many of them are attracted by the greenness of the island, and come down to recuperate after their long flight over the Atlantic. But they may also be forced to seek refuge on the island, for when thick icy fog descends, or when a northerly storm prevents flying, one sees large groups of them resting on Sandö until the bad weather has passed and they can continue on their way towards the North. When they have all left the island, barnacle geese arrive, and immediately after them the big pink-footed geese. For the latter the island is both a good resting-place after the long flight over the sea, and a fine grazing ground, to which they often return in the course of the summer, but the only permanent summer residents on the island are the sea birds.

By the end of May the ice around the island becomes so thin, in places with strong currents, that it will no longer support the weight of a man. Between about June 5 and 7 large patches of water open up to the north and south of the island, which is still, however, encircled by ice. The tides open up first cracks and then channels in this ice, and it is at this time that the sea birds start to arrive. With the frozen fjord still inaccessible to them, they sit around on the edge of the ice, watching the progress of the thaw around the places where they will later nest. Each day little parties of two or three eider-ducks fly round the island, skimming over the ice. As soon as the first patch of open water appears they take possession of it, diving down to the bottom under the ice and then coming up again. On the following day a score of other birds arrive, swim for a moment, dive, and then come out on to the ice. Then quite suddenly whole flights of eiders arrive, night and day without interruption, from the surrounding ice, and come down on the ever-widening open water. The little island, which had previously seemed such a desert, becomes the centre of life for the whole area. The vividly coloured eider drakes swim in long lines past the edge of the ice; others are asleep on the floes. Very few of them have yet paired, although the mating season is starting. Among the eiders are some long-tailed ducks and also king eiders, which are among the most impressive of all Arctic birds. They are waiting for the ice to melt on the freshwater lakes of the mainland, before leaving the island.

Sandö could not possibly accommodate all the birds which are swimming on the waters around it. Many of them will seek the estuaries of large rivers, which are already starting to thaw, while others will go to the inland lakes.

From this mass of bird life there is still one absentee, which will soon take possession of the island, and in the face of which no eider would dare to set itself up. This little bird is the Arctic tern, which flies in towards June 10, and seems to make it a point of honour to arrive on exactly the same date every year, for it is never late unless it meets a prolonged gale. The terns arrive without warning. Suddenly they are there in vast numbers, and they take possession with a great deal of noise. One can hear their harsh cries from far away on the mainland, cries which many would find disagreeable, but which bring new life to the peaceful countryside of the Arctic.

Within a few days all the birds are ready to mate. Everywhere they are courting—on the ice, in the water, and on the land. The courting males compete with persuasive calls, and parade their brilliant plumages, varying from vivid red to yellow and green, from snow-white to jet-black. The females, on the other hand, are more sombre in colour, but they manage to treat these strutting and importunate cavaliers with a certain degree of condescension, and each is followed by a number of them. Many of the male birds sound their eloquent calls, and often little fights break out between them, but the dignified eider drakes scorn such squabbling, or perhaps they just cannot be bothered. But the little long-tailed ducks are more lively, and they chase each other all round the island, trying to pull the long feathers out of their rivals' tails. These bickerings are more serious among the terns. High up in the sky the males fight duels with their long, pointed beaks. In all these quarrels it's the old story: while two males are busy fighting, a third comes in, gains the favours of the lady, and elopes with her.

The eider-duck obviously likes to be surrounded by numerous suitors, and is very successful in her efforts to attract them. I have seen up to twenty drakes following a single duck. The more numerous they are, the more interested she becomes. One way of showing her superiority is suddenly to climb out on to the ice or on to the beach; soon the whole gang of clumsy drakes are making praiseworthy efforts to follow her. Scarcely has the last drake managed to haul himself out, with a great effort, than back she goes into the water and swims off as fast as possible. Then one has the amusing sight of all the drakes falling over themselves in their efforts to be the first to catch her; but woe betide another duck who comes near! The first will quickly change from a well-mannered lady into a fury who throws herself at the intruder and chases her off.

Courtship activity goes on for some time, night and day, and the birds scarcely take time off to feed, and certainly they never sleep.

The terns remain masters of the island. With the exception of the barnacle geese, which come each day to graze along the edges of the ponds—now almost completely free of ice—no stranger has the right to go there. Those which do approach, on the ice, by water, or in the air, are soon attacked by a mob of terns which furiously chase them off. Terns will even attack man, and some sort of head covering must be worn to avoid pricks from their sharp little beaks.

By the second fortnight of June things are much quieter. The mating season is ending, and the males spend almost the whole day sleeping. The females now have only one attendant male, for the time for flirtation is over, and they are looking for a suitable place to nest. The eiders are not exacting about nesting sites, as long as the place is dry. They will use artificial shelters put up for them, or they will make their nests among pebbles on the beach, in the sand, or on gravel, or even in the interior of the island among the tussocks of grass.

Often an eider-duck will use an old nest from the preceding year. She removes any debris which has accumulated, and sometimes she will put dry grass on the bottom, but usually she lines it directly with her own down. Using her beak, she plucks enough down from her breast and belly to give the eggs a soft bedding, and she presses it all into shape with her own body. Above all, she makes sure that the nest

Page 159. *Ravens, whose survival in the most northerly regions is a measure of their intelligence.*

has a good circle of down round the rim; in fact, she puts more down round the edges than on the bottom. The whole operation scarcely takes more than two hours, and then she sits down to lay. The male is always near by, but he does not help in the preparation of the nest, and while she is laying he sits quite close to her.

The long-tailed ducks choose their nesting sites more carefully, always hiding them in grass or among stones. Their nests are smaller, and the edging of down is relatively thicker, but there is almost none at the bottom of the nest, which is lined with dry grass. The long-tailed drake prefers to have a thick rim of down around him when he is on the nest, not for warmth, but to hide the bright plumage on his belly. The down actually comes up to his shoulders when he is sitting on the nest, and if he draws in his head and neck, which he always does when disturbed, he is so well hidden that is very difficult to see him. This down is darker than that of the eider.

The terns have also started to lay, and their screams have become less frequent. They do not build anything that could be called a nest, and seem to be no more fastidious than the eiders in their choice of a site. It is enough for the ground to be dry, and wherever this is so one finds their eggs, laid in little depressions in the ground, without any lining. Terns nest from just above high-water mark on the shore up to the centre of the island, and sometimes they surround the eggs with bleached bivalve shells or small pebbles, presumably as a form of concealment. The male terns brood the eggs when the female is away feeding.

Although the terns keep a watch against intruders on the island, there is one gull which has managed to slip in among them; this is Sabine's gull, a little pilferer who allies himself with the terns and behaves as badly as they do. Perhaps this is why the terns let him in. As long as the terns are on their eggs the Sabine's gulls innocently brood their own, but as soon as the terns have to leave their nests to chase off some intruder the Sabine's gulls take the opportunity to steal

Page 160. *A long-tailed skua sitting on its eggs.*

H

the tern eggs. The terns could easily chase them off, but they seem to be unaware that they are being cheated.

The Sabine's gulls are the scientific attraction of Sandö. They are one of the rarities of bird life in Greenland, and in recent years several expeditions have visited the island to gather their eggs, which are much prized by collectors.

By the end of June all the birds are brooding, the eiders with three to six eggs, the long-tailed ducks with six to nine, while the terns have two, and more often only one. The Sabine's gulls lay two eggs, which are very similar to those of the tern. All these species spend a full twenty-four hours on the nest before flying off to feed. The eiders and the long-tailed ducks always draw the down over the eggs before leaving the nest; this serves both to hide the eggs and to maintain their temperature. Then they go off to bathe in the little ponds of fresh water, or to have a walk on the beach, and then to dive in search of food.

When the female long-tailed ducks and eiders have laid their eggs the drakes, hitherto so attentive, go into retirement; some remain close to their mates, but the majority assemble in large groups, which wander about the island and sometimes come down on the banks of the lake. Towards the beginning of July they leave the island and go off to moult elsewhere.

The incubation period of the terns lasts for fifteen to seventeen days, but the eiders brood for four weeks, and the long-tailed ducks for three weeks. The tern chicks have to remain on the island until they are fully fledged, but the ducklings of the eider and long-tailed duck are able, almost immediately after hatching, to play about on the beach, whence the mothers lead them to the waters of the fjord. The terns are thus the last to leave the island. Gradually their numbers decrease, and towards the end of their stay there are only about half as many of them as when they took possession of the island. Many have lost their eggs, and even more their chicks, which seem to be rather delicate. Nevertheless, by early August there are several hundreds of young terns ready for the long flight to the south.

From then on Sandö becomes deserted, except for a few migratory birds from father north which may stop here for a day or two. The geese have left, and the falcons have almost disappeared; a tardy long-tailed duck takes a rest on the deserted beach, and finally the last of the snow-buntings pay a brief visit to the island. Nothing remains to bear witness to the rich bird population of a month ago. The little Arctic terns, which have died prematurely, or were too weak to undertake the great flight, are devoured by glaucous gulls, and the winds have already swept the down from the nests. By October the terrible autumnal gales have started to blow. In the space of a few hours all the beaches are transformed into a chaotic desert of ice-floes. After the gales comes the frost, and then the snow, which will cover the island until, in the following year, the sun returns to make it once more a paradise for sea birds.

The Red-throated Diver

By THE middle of June all the birds have returned, and court-ship activity is at its height. Those which have gone to the extreme north have a shorter summer season, and so they have already laid, and are brooding their eggs. Once more the ground is green with the new season's plants. And one fine day, from high up in the sky, comes a loud cackling, quite different from all the other bird cries. Just below the clouds there are two birds flying side by side, with short, rapid wing-beats and extended necks. It is the red-throated diver and its mate, the last of the migratory birds to arrive, and they excel both in diving and flying. They have already paired up long before reaching the coast of Greenland, but they were prevented from coming sooner by the lack of open water. Now the little freshwater lakes are starting to thaw, and the divers have good reason for their loud calls.

We are a little north of 75° N., in the low-lying ground of Hochstetter Foreland. The two birds interrupt their regular flight to circle round over one of the numerous lakes in the area. For a moment they turn at the same height, still calling, and then descend in an ever-decreasing spiral. The wings of these fine birds are so narrow that they have to fly fast to keep airborne. Just before striking the surface they turn into wind and brake with wings fully extended, but their speed is still so great that they skim along the surface of the lake for quite a distance. Finally, they come to rest and start to look around.

With a graceful movement both birds dive and disappear for some minutes, to come up again near the bank about two yards from a tiny islet. They stop to examine the spot carefully, and then approach. In the centre of the islet there is a small depression, in which they had their nest last year. It is made of mosses and grass, and is not so high that they cannot look over the edge into it as they swim by. The divers assure themselves that all is in order. Then suddenly they stretch their necks and beat the water with their wings until there is sufficient air beneath their flight feathers to take off. After circling the lake at water-level they gain height, and once more one hears their cackling as they disappear towards the east.

There is no food for the divers in their lake, and the fjords are still blocked with ice, so in the meantime they have to hunt in the open sea, along the outer coastline, where one sees several other pairs at this time. All of them have reconnoitred their nesting sites and satisfied themselves that everything is in order, and now they will spend some time diving for small polar cod and sea-trout. Although divers are very quarrelsome and intolerant in the nesting area—each pair must have its own little lake—they seem to be more co-operative out on the fishing grounds. Each time a pair arrives, calling aloud, the others welcome it with a strident chorus which jars on the human ear. Their greetings start with a long plaintive call which goes on until the moment when the pair land on the water, and finishes with an angry miaow, which may be transcribed as *amarhuit*; this is repeated increasingly fast, and then stops quite suddenly.

It is some three days before our family of divers return to their lake, manœuvring in exactly the same way as on their first arrival. During the next week they visit the lake regularly, and spend about half the day there, but they are as quiet and secretive there as they are noisy and boisterous out on the coast, where they do most of their courtship. At

sea they can play at leisure in the clear water and display the brilliant
white of their breasts in the sun without fear of any enemy.

At the beginning of July the female is ready to lay, and starts to take
a greater interest in her islet. She returns repeatedly to examine it
minutely from every angle. Finally, with a great effort, she hauls herself out of the water on to it. Laboriously she bends the stems of the
neighbouring plants so that they form an insulating layer on which
she will lay her eggs; this is all she does in the way of making a nest.

The diver is so highly adapted for swimming that it has almost lost
the power of moving about on land. It can take off only from water,
and it would die if it came down from its usual height and had to land
on anything other than water. It comes on land only to lay and incubate
the eggs, but even this it does with some difficulty. Unlike other birds,
it is unable to stand on its toes, and so rests on the whole surface of
the feet. Its progress on land is more a crawl than a walk, and it often
has to use the wings to keep balance. That is why it always has its nest
close to the water, so that it does not have to venture far from its true
element.

The female lays two eggs in the course of a couple of days, and immediately starts to incubate them; in this she is helped by the male bird.
They relieve each other four times in the twenty-four hours, and this
allows them to fly off to the shores of the fjord, which are now ice-
free, in order to feed. They leave the nest and return to it with great
secrecy: other creatures in the neighbourhood are unaware of their
comings and goings. When one of the birds returns from the fjord it
flies in low over the nest and lands on the lake as far away from it as
possible. The other bird slips quietly off the nest and dives immediately
to come up near its mate, which then, in its turn, swims underwater
to the nest, hauls itself up, and turns the eggs over before settling down
to brood. When incubating, a diver holds its head erect, with its back
towards the sun, so that it can see better what is going on in the vicinity.
If it notices anything living, especially a man, it stretches out its neck
along the edge of the nest, so that it becomes very difficult for those
who do not know its habits to discover it at all. If it knows that it has

been discovered, or if something accidentally comes too close, it will dive noiselessly into the water and come up again as far away as possible. This manœuvre often deceives amateur egg-collectors. Occasionally a fox slinks along the shore, but the diver will remain firmly on its nest in the face of this formidable egg thief. It knows that its sharp, powerful beak is a good weapon. The fox knows this too, so he probably convinces himself that divers' eggs are too sour for his taste!

The divers regard the whole lake as their private property, and none of their fellows are allowed access. If another diver, or an innocent eider-duck or long-tailed duck, comes there to bathe, the nesting diver immediately lets out a hoarse angry warning, and rushes at the intruder, wings beating and beak at the ready. The sight of this is quite enough to remove any intruder from its domain. Only the smaller birds are allowed on the lake, and they are probably welcome because their behaviour serves to warn the diver of the approach of an enemy.

So the days and weeks pass by, until suddenly one morning the beaches of all the lakes are transformed into gardens of flowering cotton-grass. One might think that the divers had foreseen this, for their nests are placed where the cotton-grass is tallest and thickest; this is just at the time when the nests have most need of concealment, for the closer it is to hatching time, the more the divers have to remain on the nest, without leaving the eggs except in extreme danger. They increase their vigilance, and come and go without displacing the cotton-grass.

The red-throated diver is scarcely ever hunted. It can easily defend itself against the small animals, and the large carnivores rarely come to the areas where it nests. Its only real enemy is man, whom it knows from the southern lands where it spends the winter. This is probably why the sight of men passing along the edge of the lake makes the divers more watchful than they would otherwise need to be.

After four weeks of incubation a small crack appears in one of the eggs, and a moment later a chick pops its head out and announces its arrival with a repeated "pip, pip." The brooding parent spreads its wings carefully over the edge of the nest to conserve the heat, so that the little one may dry as soon as possible. One of the parents is always at the nest until the last chick has hatched. For a time the care of their helpless offspring makes them forget their former secrecy and watchfulness, and when they relieve each other, to keep the chicks warm, they do so in the open and quite near to the nest. Nothing will make them leave their offspring. In the face of any enemy, even man, they will raise their sharp beaks and hiss menacingly. If the enemy is persistent the bird will call its mate, which flies in and lands, close to the nest, hissing loudly.

The young start to be fed on the day after hatching. Their food consists of very small codling caught in the nearest fjord; the parents fill their crop with these and regurgitate them into the mouths of the chicks. The young are kept in the nest for only three days, but they are unable to reach the water by themselves, and have to be helped by the parents. This may occasionally happen on the third day if the diver suddenly sees a man coming along the shore towards the nest. At first it tries the usual method of stretching out its neck and remaining motionless until the danger has passed, but if this is not successful it takes a quick decision and rushes into the water, at the same time pushing the chicks over the edge of the nest. One of them falls on its back into the water, but quickly regains its balance and swims quite naturally towards the parent. The other chick has only reached the edge, where it is perched precariously, and then falls back into the nest and lies there motionless and hidden among the cotton-grass. In spite of the indignant protests of the diver, the man has come right up to the nest. He bends down, picks up the chick, and puts it in the water. It also swims quite naturally, which is astonishing for an infant only three days old. With its second chick close by, the diver stops hissing and becomes less aggressive. It swims away with the two chicks following valiantly in its wake, and never returns to the nest. Early the next day one of the divers is out in the middle of the lake, with the chicks sleeping on its back. A little later the other parent returns from the fjord, with its crop filled with delicious little fishes. As usual it flies in over the surface and lands close to its mate. The chicks slide into the water and gobble up the fish, which the parent disgorges for them.

The divers now have an enemy which is more persistent than those they have hitherto encountered. This is the long-tailed skua, a clever and insolent rascal, who always arrives without warning. He will try to attack the young divers when they are separated from their parents, but the latter know well the danger which is gliding down on to their inoffensive offspring, and take good care to keep close to them. Sometimes the skua tries to scatter the young by frightening them. After a turn round the lake he will disappear, and then return unexpectedly, coming in so low that his wing-tips almost touch the ground. He quickly gains height, and then swoops down on the family when they are least expecting him. The chicks are terrified, but a beak, sharp as a dagger, flashes out like lightning, and the attacker has to make a quick turn in order to escape.

The chicks are able to dive from the time they leave the nest, and in this way they can escape from their enemies at a very tender age, and, what is also important, they can partly relieve their parents from the continuous task of searching for food. The chicks catch little crustaceans, and in the waters near the fjord there are masses of sea-trout fry which they find an easy prey.

The ability to fly comes as the last stage in their development. They cannot, of course, leave the lake until they have learnt to fly. Towards the end of August, after several more or less successful attempts, they are able to get into the air with their parents and to fly to the shores of the fjord. Henceforth the young have to be self-supporting. The links between them and their parents become more and more tenuous, until they are finally severed during the migration to the South, where they will spend the winter under kinder skies.

In the red-throated diver there is no external difference between the sexes, and both may vary considerably in size. In my observations of the pair described above I was never sure which was the male and which was the female. One was a little larger than the other, but the main difference was in their behaviour. The smaller bird was astonishingly timid, and would escape to the water at the slightest excuse, while the larger one would always remain on the nest until the last moment. I should add that the birds were not aware of my presence near the nest. In order to find out how they behaved in the face of an enemy, I got one of my companions to walk along the edge of the lake, while I was concealed in my hide. In this way I was able to observe their reactions to man.

In general both birds were equally conscientious in their incubation duties, but the larger bird showed itself much more interested in the care of the eggs and later of the chicks. If chased off the nest it would return as soon as the danger had passed, whereas the smaller bird would remain on the lake and call until its mate came up, which usually happened immediately, and only then would it return to the nest.

On several occasions the smaller bird was absent for a whole day, and then the larger one would be away for only half an hour at a time before returning to incubate the eggs. This difference between them in their desire to incubate became more apparent towards the end of the incubation period. After the eggs had hatched the larger bird gave far more attention to the chicks, and so I presumed that it was the female. In order to be quite sure I later killed it, and was surprised to find that it was, in fact, the male. So as not to judge from a single case I also made observations on other pairs of red-throated divers. In all of these the males incubated the eggs and attended to the young much more conscientiously than the females. I also found that the female will stop incubating if the male is killed, whereas if the female disappears the male continues to brood the eggs and feed the chicks.

The Geese of the High North

MOST OF the Arctic birds are almost tame, or at any rate much more so than those anywhere else, but this cannot be said of the geese. In my attempts to observe their everyday life I always found them extremely shy and distrustful. Their wintering in temperate countries has taught them how dangerous man can be, and this innate distrust remains with them, even in areas which are quite safe. Although in Greenland they are scarcely more subject to attack than any of the other birds, they always remain on the watch, and warn each other of anything going on in the neighbourhood.

There are four species of goose in North-east Greenland—the white-fronted, the brent, the barnacle, and the pink-footed. The white-fronted goose occurs only exceptionally, and as far as I know it has been seen there only on one occasion. This was a female killed during the autumn migration by a Greenlander at the mouth of Scoresby Sound. Probably it had lost its way and arrived in East Greenland instead of Iceland or some other place; the species does, however, breed in West Greenland.

The brent geese are common migrants, but are known to breed only in a few places in Greenland, and even there in small numbers. It is, however, believed that there must be large colonies of brent geese somewhere in the north-east, for every spring immense numbers of them arrive along the coast. They do not, however, settle down in any place easily accessible to man, and it is thought that they must be making for Northern Greenland. All the same, this does not explain how such an essentially herbivorous bird prefers to live in areas so poor in vegetation.

On the other hand, the barnacle and the pink-footed goose breed in large numbers in North-east Greenland. The barnacle has the wider distribution, and extends farther to the north, while the pink-footed goose lives mainly in the southern part of the region, between Scoresby Sound and Hudson Land.

These two birds, always on the watch, form one of the most characteristic features of the Arctic summer. The novice who comes to Greenland and sees innumerable geese, hears them calling, and finds their tracks everywhere, naturally expects to discover their nests. In actual fact many trappers have lived here for years without finding a single one, although they have searched for the tasty eggs during the nesting season. The suggestion that they nest on steep, rocky escarpments seems odd to anyone who judges Arctic bird life from his knowledge of the birds in temperate regions. Gulls and guillemots are known to nest on rocky ledges, but the goose lives on flat plains. In spite of this the little barnacle goose does prefer to perch its nest on an inaccessible cliff, often almost at the summit of mountains situated far in the interior of the country, where no other bird goes.

It had been thought likely that the barnacle goose did not breed under the same conditions as other geese, but it was not until the time of the Danmark Expedition that the true facts were elucidated. The eminent Danish ornithologist A. L. V. Manniche had already spent two years in Greenland, before he first found one of the large colonies of barnacle geese in Germania Land. His account of this discovery is so lively and interesting that I will give it in his own words:

On June 8 and 9 I had, for the first time, an opportunity to observe barnacle geese on their own ground. In an area of lakes and marshes, far in the interior of the country, to the north of the big Lake of Seals, and six to nine miles from the nearest sea-water, the barnacle geese were leading a pleasant life, and one which quite astonished me. The vegetation of the marshy land was lush. The Arctic willow, as well as other plants, grew profusely. Although still early in the season, the snow which had already melted formed numerous ponds, which gave the place an added attraction for swimming and wading birds. This unusually early thaw was almost certainly caused by the action of the strong sun on the dark peaty soil.

On my arrival the barnacle geese were standing in pairs and small groups in pools of water, or were grazing near by, some of them even high up on the sides of the mountain. At fixed times of the day and night the geese left the marsh and disappeared in a southerly direction towards the highest and most central part of Three Crowns Mountain. Thinking that there might be a large lake near this mountain to which the geese repaired after feeding, I walked over in the direction taken by them. There I found two large freshwater lakes, in which there were only a few geese, which flew off in alarm farther into the mountain. About half a mile farther on I found the answer to the problem. Along the whole length of the great mountain-side there were barnacle geese flying back and forward like bees round a hive, and a continuous humming, which sounded more like distant, muffled chatter, greeted my ears. Sitting at the foot of the mountain, I spent some hours watching the geese. With my field-glasses, I could pick out every detail without difficulty. Some of the geese flew up and down along the sides of the mountain, and sometimes so high into the air that they went over the top and disappeared on the other side, but the majority sat, usually in pairs, on ledges on the mountain-side, some of which seemed so small that there was scarcely room for the pair, let alone for a nest. The geese were only on the most central, vertical, and completely bare part of the mountain-face, and never lower than about 600 feet from the bottom. As the place was quite inaccessible I fired some shots against the cliff to scare the geese, in the hope of getting some idea of the size of the colony. About 150 birds returned to their homes. So far as I could make out egg-laying had not yet started.

After the discovery of this colony it was not difficult to find others. We now know all the colonies in the area between Scoresby Sound and Germania Land. The geese that nest in the interior of the country must have stretches of fresh water not far away. On the coast, where they also nest in certain places, they establish themselves in the middle of gull colonies.

Naturally I wanted to see the nests themselves. At Scoresby Sound I had tried to reach them on several occasions, either by climbing or by being lowered on a rope from above, but this was an extremely dangerous process, and, as I only had primitive equipment, I did not go on with it. It was not until the spring of 1932 that I saw a colony of barnacle geese near Clavering Island, in a place that was not completely inaccessible. This was a small island in Tyrol Fjord, just off the north coast of Clavering Island. The southern part of the island rose gradually to a height of 600 feet, and then fell perpendicular to the sea. The barnacle geese had their nests on ledges on the cliff face, and, according to some trappers who had been on the island the previous year, it was possible to climb down to the nests.

On the 11th of June, by which time I thought that the geese would have started to lay, I went to the island with the trapper Larsen from Sandodden, crossing the fjord which was still covered with ice. During the journey and even on our arrival on the island we saw not a single goose. As we walked along the ridge of the island we came across a colony of glaucous gulls, with about thirty-five pairs. Their nests were all inaccessible, and some were so small that the head and tail of the incubating bird projected over the edge; from the top of the cliff we could look right down into these nests.

As always happens when a stranger approaches a colony of gulls, the birds were soon all around us, screaming harshly. Some swept down low over our heads, while others circled high up under the clouds. As soon as they saw us leaving their territory they came down one by one, and settled again on their nests. We then passed a cliff face which was split by a number of crevices. On each side of the precipice the face was smooth and there were no birds, but about 300 feet below us we could see a ledge with a nesting barnacle goose. In spite of the distance it immediately stood up and flew off. With field-glasses we could see four eggs in the nest, which was made entirely of down. A little farther on another goose flew off its nest, which was in a hole in the cliff, so that we could see only part of it. Then we came to three long ledges, with gaps in several places. The highest ledge was between twenty to forty feet below the top edge of the cliff, and in several places it was large enough to take a man. It was obvious that this was the main part of the colony, and as we appeared the males took off. The incubating females waited for some minutes, turning their heads to watch us, and then joined the males and flew with them along the cliff face. We walked along the whole length of the cliff to determine the size of the colony, and counted thirty-six pairs, but the astonishing thing was the variation in the number of eggs in the nests. Half of them had five or six eggs, while the others had seven or eight, except for one nest which had fifteen. This nest probably belonged to two families, which is not unusual among geese.

Larsen helped me to descend on a rope to one of the nests. The eggs were resting in a natural cavity, and were surrounded by a circle of down and small feathers, without any other material. The nest was crawling with fleas; when I touched the down I immediately had a score of them on my hand. The larvæ of these fleas were living in the guano which was abundant all round the nest. The adult fleas seemed not only to have the job of tormenting the brooding bird, but also appeared to be doing a service to the nest, for the eggs, which could not have been more than four or five days old, were already so covered with the excrement of the fleas as to appear brown, instead of the original white. This was certainly an unusual method of camouflage.

As long as we remained on the rock, up above their nests, the geese flew up and down along the face of the cliff, just out of range of a gun. Once we had gone, they surveyed the area where we had been, to make sure that we had not hidden ourselves, and then returned to their nests.

In order to take a close-up photograph of a goose on its nest—naturally this was only possible with a telephoto lens—I had to hide for nearly an hour among some rocks on the edge of the cliff. Although I was at least ninety feet from her, this goose was so shy that when she finally returned to her nest I only just had time to take the picture before she flew off again.

When one knows the inaccessible nesting sites of the barnacle goose and when one has seen its goslings, at an age of only a few days, trotting along the edge of a pond or on the sandy shore of a fjord, one wonders how these tiny creatures, with minute wings still hidden in down, have managed to descend from such perilous heights. I cannot really give a completely satisfactory answer. Nevertheless, one day in Hurry Inlet I saw two barnacle geese flying down from a high escarpment. Both of them were carrying something in their beaks, which we identified with field-glasses as their own goslings. These they deposited on the edge of a pond. We hastened towards the spot and found two goslings, which immediately fled out on to the water with the old birds. From this single observation, however, one cannot be certain that barnacle geese always bring their young down from the mountains in this way. Other observers have seen small goslings jump down from the nesting ledges, but this was always in places where there was water at the foot of the cliff. Sometimes they come down from a height of 600, 900, or even 1200 feet, and one would think that they must be killed by the roughness of the cliff, in spite of their lightness and the covering of down. Besides, they must be an easy prey for the ravens, gulls, and skuas which are always on the look-out. This is still one of the unanswered problems in the life history of the barnacle goose.

For a long time we did not know the breeding-places of the pink-footed geese. This is because they build their nests in the most remote places, particularly in the interior of sheltered fjords, and on large sandy deltas near the mouths of rivers, which are surrounded on all sides by deep running water. They make their nests on hillocks of dry sand. Even if such places are more accessible than rocky cliffs the incubating birds are still well protected against their enemies, for the thaw is at its height and the water is rushing down in torrents, so they are isolated not only from the majority of animals, but also from man.

I was fortunate to be the first to discover one of the Greenland colonies of pink-footed geese. Some Greenlanders from Scoresby Sound told me that during a journey at the beginning of June they had seen some large geese on the east coast of Jameson Land, in the region of Hurry Inlet. The geese were assembled on a wide beach, and some of their nests contained freshly laid eggs. I reckoned that they were referring to Point Constable, in Hurry Inlet. In the autumn of the same year I passed this place on a boat journey to Klitdalen, and took the opportunity to pay a short visit. By this time the geese were ready to leave the country, and so I could not expect to find them on the nesting-grounds. I saw their tracks, but nothing remained of the nests except some small excavations in the sand. The down had been blown away by the wind.

At the beginning of June in the following year I returned to the great delta at Point Constable, but it proved extremely difficult to reach the place where the geese were nesting. During the journey we had great trouble in getting the sledge over the ice, which was already flooded with water from the melting snow, and we often found ourselves faced with torrents, which seemed to be bottomless. The waters were coming down so fast that they would splash us up to the waist if we so much as put in a foot. For a long time we searched for a ford, until one of the party—we were three—suddenly disappeared in the icy waters. Having rescued him, we continued on our way, completely soaked. It was one of the most difficult trips I have ever made in summer, and it took us twenty-four hours. On several occasions we had to wade waist-high in the ice-cold water; but we found the geese. They were in a relatively small area which was free of snow, and intersected by innumerable little streams. The birds stood in pairs on the summits of the sandy knolls, which were a characteristic feature of the inner part of the delta. We tried to creep up to them by hiding behind the knolls, each of which was about six feet high, but as soon as they lost sight of us they would quickly fly off and silently glide away, almost

I

at ground-level. They would then climb and turn back towards us with a loud cackle. There were about fifty birds in the group. Under protest from them, we continued our search and found some thirty nests in all. One of the nests was on the edge of a lagoon, but all the others were perched on the hillocks of sand, with the eggs lying on a bed of down and dry grass. In most of the nests the circle of down round the edge had been pulled over the eggs, in exactly the same way as the eider-ducks do. The number of eggs varied from one to seven, so the geese were only about half-way through their egg-laying. Some of the nests had been looted, one by a fox and others by wolves. Judging by the tracks, the colony had been visited, not later than the previous night, by two wolves which had destroyed a number of nests. On the following day we saw the wolves coming down from the high ground behind the colony, presumably to continue their thieving, but they fled as soon as they saw us. These formidable thieves could not have reached the colony without suffering an ice-bath, but this inconvenience, which led to one of us spending a week in bed, did not seem to deter them from seeking the big, tasty goose eggs.

During the following days I tried to watch the geese on their nests, but all attempts to get them to ignore my hide were in vain. They preferred to leave their eggs rather than risk the slightest danger. The fact that, in spite of this, I am able to show on page 135 two photographs of pink-footed geese is due solely to one of those lucky chances which sooner or later favour all animal photographers. I was in a hide on the edge of a little stream formed by the melting snow, in a high valley on Wollaston Foreland, watching a sanderling which was sitting on her eggs right in front of me. There were several goose colonies down on the coast, and some of the birds were in the habit of coming up to this place to graze. I often heard them flying over my hide on their way to and from the nesting-grounds, but I never dreamt that one would land near me. I was therefore astonished, to say the least, when I suddenly saw two geese land on the edge of the stream, not more than sixty feet from the hide. They stopped cackling as soon as they landed, and started to look around. Then they began to graze, and I took my first picture, without them having seen me. They even gave me time to change the ordinary lens for a telephoto, and I had just taken a close-up photograph when one of the geese spotted the hide. But when they flew off I was in possession of the rarest of all my Greenland bird photographs.

Birds of the Uplands

O N A SUMMER journey in North-east Greenland you will meet a number of small birds which are hard at work trying to attract your attention. In particular there are two small waders which literally walk about between your feet, and seem to have no fear. One of these is the ringed plover, which has a distinctive white band round the neck, and although it is smaller than a starling you cannot help noticing it. As soon as it sees you it immediately gives a piping call and flies up to welcome you. Still piping, it hops away at great speed on its long, thin legs, carefully making sure that you are following. In a few minutes a number of its companions are attracted by its continuous piping, and soon you have in front of you a whole crowd of these talkative little creatures. Naturally they all have their nests and young in the vicinity, and the whole performance is but a ruse to lead you away from their territory. If, in spite of their efforts, you come too near a nest—which is so difficult to see that you only rarely find one—the birds become so scared, lest you tread on it, that they will go so far as to risk their own lives by throwing themselves in front of your feet. Their behaviour is so peculiar that you immediately stop. With wings apparently broken, the nesting pair drag themselves pitifully along the ground, and if they

pass a little hollow in the ground they will flap their wings as though
in pain. They also manage to make their plumage as obvious as possible, spreading the tail like a fan so that its white transverse bar is
clearly seen, and falling on their side so that the white belly flashes in the
sun. All this is done so that you will try to catch them, or at least to
follow them, and in this way they lead you away from the nest. As
soon as this danger is over the birds quickly return to normal and
mingle with the other plovers which are trotting in front of you,
merrily piping. When you are sufficiently far from the nest the pair that
have been so active retire discreetly. You always think that you have the
same pair in front of you, but, in fact, the first you met have long been
replaced by others through whose territory you are now walking.

The other small wader is the sanderling, which also makes a point
of being noticed, although less blatantly. It has a brownish-grey
plumage, and always runs along the ground as though leaning forward,
with rapid movements which resemble those of a mouse. It breeds near
to the ringed plovers, and when the latter give warning of the approach
of an intruder the sanderling surreptitiously leaves its nest and runs
away in a zigzag course over the ground. Then it flies off and appears,
as though by chance, among the plovers, which are busily occupied
in searching for food. Once the intruder has gone, the sanderling flies
back to where it first took off. There it again busies itself in looking for
food, until it quickly and almost invisibly creeps back to the nest. The
dark plumage and rapid movements make it very difficult to follow
by eye. Just as you spot it against the dull patterns of the soil it suddenly
disappears, and you find it again twenty yards away, sitting on its
eggs. If you take it by surprise on the nest it will behave like a ringed
plover and entice you away.

Although these two species live in the same locality and often feed
together, they choose very different places for their nests. The ringed
plovers lay their eggs on bare stony or gravelly ground, devoid of
vegetation. The only materials they appear to need are pebbles, particularly the round siliceous ones, which are astonishingly similar to
their own eggs. Such pebbles form the only bedding for their eggs.

The sanderling, on the other hand, needs a dark soil with plants, which will blend with its plumage. Its eggs are almost green, and they rest on leaves among the vegetation. The nest itself consists of a thin layer of leaves of the willow and other plants, placed at the bottom of a small depression in the ground. On the fjaeldmark of North-east Greenland—that is, the dry stony slopes which make up the greater part of this region—the earth is mottled dark and light, according to the presence of more or less vegetation. These conditions allow the two birds, which have such different requirements for nesting sites, to breed quite close to each other.

During incubation the plovers are lively and active, and not easily put out by difficulties. Often, when I have been watching a nest at close quarters, the female has finally given up trying to draw me away, but has not dared to return to her eggs. She may have advanced towards them several times, only to retreat at the last moment. The male, who has been watching this scene, will lose patience and, with a great show of anger, will push the female towards the nest. After she has finally refused to return he will quietly go and sit on it, without showing the slightest fear, even though I may be only a yard away; nor is he afraid of the big eye of the camera watching him at even closer range. There are considerable differences between individual ringed plovers in their attitude to the nest. I have seen some which just would not return as long as I was there, but it is rare for them to abandon the eggs completely.

In the sanderling we do not know whether both sexes take turns in incubating, or whether one has sole charge of this task. If it were not that some observations made in Greenland and in other Arctic regions were contrary to my own I would assert that it is the females which incubate. All the birds which I have had to kill on the nest, in order to clear up this question, were females; the males always remained at some distance from the nest. A. L. V. Manniche came to the same conclusion in Germania Land. Others, however, affirm that the male also incubates (a frequent occurrence in waders). It is difficult to find the truth, for both sexes look alike, and so one is reduced to killing a large number of birds on the nest, which is very undesirable.

Near its nest the sanderling is one of the most congenial birds I know. Once it has grasped the idea that it can no longer hope to draw you away, it gets used to being watched and sits on its eggs right in front of you. If your visits are repeated at short intervals it will remain quite confidently on the nest. From my daily visits I have gained the confidence of a sanderling to the point of being able to sit alongside it, without its making any movement other than turning its head towards me.

Ringed plovers and sanderlings incubate their eggs for three weeks. Their chicks have strong, outsize feet, which allow them to run about on the pebbly ground from their second day, and to catch flies, midges, and spiders. The day after hatching one of the parents takes them under its wings to warm them up and so dry them quickly. By the second day the nest is already too small for them, and they start to leave it and crawl away to find a larger hiding-place in the vicinity. The little sanderlings are astonishingly clever at concealing themselves among the willow branches, while the young ringed plovers remain in among the stones, which they resemble so closely that it needs a sharp eye to discover them. On the third day they can stand up and move about in the vicinity, but the parents keep an eye on them, for they are still far from being independent.

The sanderling removes its young if they are threatened by danger. I confirmed this after having ringed some chicks which were scarcely a day old. They were in a willow-bush not far from the nest, and were not yet able to stand up. I put the rings on in the afternoon. The same evening, while walking along about half a mile away I found a new nest. As I prepared to ring the chicks in it I saw that they had already been ringed. They were, in fact, the same birds I had ringed six hours before on the beach. They could not have made such a long journey by themselves, for they were unable to walk. They must, therefore, have been brought there by the parents, which doubtless carried out this feat in the same way as does a woodcock, which can transport its young one by one in its beak.

The helplessness of these young birds obliges them to live hidden away; but their pitiful piping and the anxiety of their parents betray them. Sometimes one suddenly comes across a little being fluttering its midget wings, and fleeing in front of you to disappear suddenly behind some stones, or to crouch in the bottom of a small hole. From an age of one week they already run fast enough to escape from most dangers without the aid of their parents. Then their wings start to develop, and they are able to fly from the third or fourth week after hatching.

Young waders have innumerable enemies. Among the mammals the ermine is perhaps the most formidable. By night it methodically explores all sorts of terrain. Even if its principal goal is the lemming, it will also devour chicks too weak to escape, and so will the snowy owl and the falcon, for which a tiny chick must be but a single mouthful. The ravens, and particularly the greedy glaucous gulls, also hunt chicks as an agreeable change from their usual menu. But the most terrible enemy of all is the long-tailed skua. This is the same bird that I have spoken of in the chapter on the red-throated diver—a brigand, who watches for his prey from afar, and swoops down and kills it by surprise. For hours at a time he can remain motionless on a small hillock or rock, keeping watch all round. Nothing escapes his keen eye, and the slightest movements of the young birds attract his attention. Soon, with wings vibrating, he will descend on the victim exactly like a bird of prey, or he may patrol his hunting area, flying silently and low over the ground. Nobody sees him until he is there, and then it is too late to escape. The adult waders are always on their guard against this predator, and the smaller species, such as ringed plover and sanderling, are no match for him. Even if they group together and mob him they do not always succeed in avoiding the penalty. Only the energetic and noisy turnstones seem to be able to chase him off their territory. You often see a skua followed by a group of turnstones, which force him to fly higher and higher until finally he makes up his mind to go away.

The long-tailed skua itself nests right on the ground, and defends its eggs furiously against any other bird, and even against man. If one can forget its rapacity one must admire the grace and elegance of a bird which is one of the adornments of the bleak Arctic countryside.

Index

References to illustrations are in italics